LONE STAR JUSTICE

LONE STAR JUSTICE

A BIOGRAPHY OF
JUSTICE TOM C. CLARK

BY EVAN A. YOUNG

Hendrick-Long Publishing Co.

txr

LONE STAR JUSTICE
A BIOGRAPHY OF JUSTICE TOM C. CLARK

Hendrick-Long Publishing Company
P.O. Box 25123
Dallas, Texas 75225

Library of Congress Cataloging-in-Publication Data

Young, Evan A.
Lone star justice: a biography of Tom C. Clark / by Evan A. Young
    p. cm.
Includes bibliographical references and index.
Summary: Introduces the life and times of the only Texan to have served as a justice of the United States Supreme Court.
ISBN 1-885777-11-6 (alk. paper)
1. Clark, Tom C. (Tom Campbell). 1899-1977. 2. Judges—United States—Biography—Juvenile literature. [Clark, Tom C. (Tom Campbell), 1899-1977. 2. Judges. 3. Youths' writings.]
I. Title.
KF8746.C54Y68 1998
347.763'2634—dc21
[b]   98-16575
                                                                CIP
                                                                 AC

Photographs from the Tom C. Clark Papers reproduced with the permission of the Tarlton Law Library, University of Texas at Austin.

ISBN: 1-885777-11-6

COVER AND INTERIOR DESIGN: DIANNE NELSON, SHADOW CANYON GRAPHICS

PRINTED AND BOUND IN THE UNITED STATES OF AMERICA

For the students and faculty of

Tom C. Clark High School,

who continue to bring honor

to the name of Tom C. Clark.

CONTENTS

PREFACE

Tom C. Clark, as one of few to reach the nation's highest court, has been subjected to a fate that in history is almost worse than infamy: he has been ignored.

Many students of Supreme Court history will recognize his name and perhaps know a few of the opinions he wrote, but scarcely any know much about *him*. For Texans, he is especially significant; no other born and bred Texan has sat upon the Supreme Court of the United States.

Northside Independent School District, in San Antonio, Texas, names all of its high schools after justices of the Supreme Court. Justice Clark knew of the honor of having a school named for him; a year before he died, when construction on the school was just beginning, he wrote a postcard to the superintendent of schools in the Northside Independent School District—now on display in the main office of Tom C. Clark High School—which says that "such an honor . . . makes my cup runneth over."

Justice Clark died before his school opened. But his son, former Attorney General Ramsey Clark, along with Clark's widow, Mary, his daughter, Mimi Clark Gronlund, and family friend Lady Bird Johnson, attended the dedication ceremony.

When I served as president of the National Honor Society (NHS) at Tom C. Clark High School I was responsible for organizing the induction ceremony for new members: I had to find a guest speaker and choose a theme for the ceremony. In my case, the two melted into one. As an intern in the office of Bexar County Judge Cyndi Taylor Krier—a much sought after speaker—I decided to ask the judge to give our keynote speech. She agreed. She remarked that in other NHS ceremonies in which she had spoken she had incorporated elements from the lives of the school's namesake into her discussion of the ideals of NHS: service, character, leadership, and scholarship.

That would have been easy had our school been named for Thomas Edison or Thomas Jefferson, but our namesake was Thomas Clark. Judge Krier made me realize that the mistake of Justice Clark's obscurity was something that should be rectified for as many people associated with the school and our state as possible.

Tom C. Clark became the center of the National Honor Society induction for 1994. The NHS historian, Andrea Tews, drew an impressive portrait of Justice Clark for the cover of our program, and I wrote a brief biography of him for an insert in the program. Judge Krier's speech was full of anecdotes about Justice Clark's life. Most important, the National Honor Society established the first-ever permanent award for juniors: the Justice Clark Award. This prize, given to the single junior each year who best exemplifies the qualities of service, leadership, scholarship, and character, will be a long-lasting reminder of the life and service of our school's namesake.

When Katsy Morris, my senior English teacher, allowed each student to choose any topic that he or she wanted for the senior project, the choice was clear: I would continue my journey to discover the man who gave our school its name. My research for Judge Krier and my senior project are the origins of this text.

The purpose of this book is not to present an exhaustive biography or critical history concerning Tom C. Clark; rather it is to acquaint the people—and especially the students—of Texas with a fellow Texan who has helped change our world.

If anyone deserves to be in the pantheon of great Texans, using any criterion, Justice Clark does. History should not forget Tom C. Clark . . . the Lone Star Justice.

ACKNOWLEDGEMENTS

I can thank no one more than Mimi Clark Gronlund. She has offered tremendous support ever since she learned of my project and has provided me with important information that I would otherwise never have found. Without her help, this book would have only a fraction of whatever value it now has.

Many people have helped in many ways. Many thanks to Bexar County Judge Cyndi Taylor Krier for providing the idea of researching Justice Clark—without her request for information about him I would have never started writing. I greatly appreciate the extra energy and kind encouragement of Mike Widener, archivist and rare books librarian at the University of Texas Tarlton Law Library, for his help in working with Justice Clark's papers and in obtaining the photographs. Thanks to Katsy Morris for encouragement at the early stages and to Jerry Daniel for providing pictures and information about the opening of Tom C. Clark High School. I appreciate the help and friendliness of Phyllis Giffin, principal of Tom C. Clark High School, who provided access to useful primary sources about Justice Clark. I thank Kathleen Shurtleff of the Supreme Court Historical Society for providing reference material and Attorney Bill Nash for his help in understanding legal principles. I am very grateful to Bonnie Ellison, of the Northside Independent School District, for her crucial help in getting the book published.

CHAPTER ONE

EARLY LIFE

People born into rapidly changing times often act as forces of change themselves. The year 1899 is not generally considered a year that engulfed the United States in a significant amount of turbulence; a conflict with Spain had just been resolved, President William McKinley was leading the country in a fairly conservative direction, and across America big business was exerting its enormous power.

Perhaps this age of cautious change helps explain why a little boy born in Dallas, Texas, on September 23, 1899, would pursue change at a hesitant and conservative pace when he would become a justice of the U.S. Supreme Court fifty years later.

Thomas Campbell Clark, son of William Henry Clark and Jennie Falls Clark, was born into a family that had long been established in the Democratic Party and the legal profession of Texas. His father was a prominent Dallas attorney who had been elected the youngest president of the Texas Bar Association. It seemed natural, then, for Tom to hope to someday follow in the footsteps of his elders and become a lawyer.

Tom's family, once quite wealthy, experienced difficult times financially. And like many elite families, they were not immune to the problems that plagued millions of other Americans. Clark's daughter, writing about her father's early life, described the effects of one of this century's most devastating social issues. William Clark, the great lawyer and political figure, became an alcoholic; eventually his addiction drowned out the honorable and admirable aspects of his life and career, bringing his family into serious financial difficulties.

Tom earned money by working in a drugstore and as a newspaper delivery boy; he helped his mother do chores, such as milking the cows and tending the vegetable garden (for which he earned a medal). But Tom didn't have to work all the time; he was an outdoorsman—enjoying fishing, hunting, and physical exercise. He became one of America's first Eagle Scouts. Somehow he found the time to be a voracious reader, and he also maintained high standards in his school work. He became an especially good orator and won numerous awards in debate. Even at this young age, Clark has been described as a "workaholic." His efforts to help his mother, improve himself, and earn money indicate well-developed senses of duty, honor, and devotion to family.

Clark was ready to begin training to enter the profession of his father and grandfather. However, World War I interrupted his education. In the first half of this century, it was expected that all young men would serve their country in times of war. Tom Clark was no exception. In 1917 he graduated from Bryan High School in Dallas and enrolled in the Virginia Military Institute in preparation for the service. But his family could not afford the expense; Clark dropped out after a year and enlisted in the Texas National Guard to do his share in the war. He never left Texas during his brief time in the service.

But World War I soon ended, and Clark left the military to pursue his education. After returning home, Clark had to choose between the new Southern Methodist University in

Clark was an avid Boy Scout and later one of the nation's first Eagle Scouts. Shown here in uniform about 1910, age ten or eleven.

FROM THE TOM C. CLARK PAPERS, TARLTON LAW LIBRARY, UNIVERSITY OF TEXAS AT AUSTIN

Dallas (SMU) and the University of Texas at Austin. Clark's daughter, Mimi, later wrote that he originally had planned to attend SMU, which was then only a few years old. It would have been cheaper because it was in Dallas and Clark could have lived at home. However, staying home did not appeal to Clark; he therefore chose to enroll at the University of Texas. He had one advantage in Austin: his older brother, Bill, was already there.

In 1921 Clark earned a bachelor of arts degree. Incredibly, it took him only two years, far less than today's usual four. Perhaps even more surprising, Clark earned his law degree from the University of Texas only a year later. He was well on his way to continuing the family tradition.

At the university, Clark met Mary Ramsey, whose father had been a candidate for governor and who had served on the two highest courts in Texas: the Supreme Court and the Court of Criminal Appeals. It wasn't love at first sight, at least for Mary. The first time she saw Tom was from a window in her boarding house in Austin; her roommate, who was dating Bill Clark, pointed to him and said, "That's Bill's brother." Mary had no reaction besides thinking that he seemed rather skinny.

Her opinion of Tom changed as they came to know each other. Their story is not very different from many other couples'. Both Tom and Mary dated a number of people, but situations presented themselves (often with some effort on Tom's part) in which they could develop a special relationship.

The two dated from early 1922 until the summer of 1924, when they became engaged. During this time, they had their ups and downs—just as all couples do. Mary would later say that her feelings for Tom were nurtured by his notes to her. "He wrote beautiful love letters," she commented.[1] He wrote to her every day when she was in California during the summer of 1923; in 1924, when she was again in California, he called her frequently and, again, wrote every day. His chivalrous behavior convinced Mary that she and Tom were right for each other.

They were married on November 8, 1924, while Clark was still a beginning lawyer, practicing in Dallas in his father and brother's firm. It was tough living at first—but as newlyweds starting out in life, it didn't seem overly tough to them. Clark had one steady client, a man who owned a barbecue stand, who gave him five dollars a week. Tom kept busy trying to build up his law practice. And since he and Mary lived in Dallas, they were able to see their families frequently.

In 1925, the Clarks had the first of their three children, Tom C. Jr. This was delightful for Tom; he loved children and, as his daughter later said, he "was an overindulgent father" who enjoyed giving things to his children, being with them, and doing things with them. In 1927 the Clarks had another son, William Ramsey (who would be called Ramsey). Two years after Ramsey's birth, the Clarks moved outside the city limits to a small farm that Tom had purchased.

In February 1932 a parent's worst nightmare came true for Tom and Mary when Tom Jr. contracted spinal meningitis and died at the age of six. This tragic loss caused Tom incalculable pain and nearly destroyed Mary, but they endured. The portrait of their little boy hangs to this day in the Clarks' apartment in Washington, D.C., where Mary still lives. Not long after Tom Jr.'s death, the Clarks' daughter Mildred (who would be called Mimi) was born in 1933. This blessing, while certainly not erasing the pain of Tom Jr.'s death, at least made it more bearable.

* * *

Young attorneys have an advantage if they can leave law school and immediately enter a secure job. Clark's father and brother had a law firm in Dallas. Tom joined them in 1922 and began his lifelong association with leaders in the legal and political arenas.

A job as civil district attorney for Dallas County presented itself to Clark, due largely to his family's political ties, and he was appointed to the position by the Dallas County Commissioners Court. He was working with elected District Attorney William McCraw.

Working for the county provided Clark three important benefits. First, it gave him the experience he would need later in managing a large legal establishment. Since civil law concerns itself with such things as taxes, property foreclosures, and claims against the government, Clark gained valuable training as a lawyer able to supervise not only himself but also numerous other attorneys.

Second, Clark learned how to operate efficiently and effectively in the courthouse, another essential job for any attorney. He went into courtrooms every day, and it is said that he never lost a case; he once remarked that "a good lawyer doesn't file a case unless he's sure he'll win."[2] The contact he made with judges, as well as the tactics he learned as a courtroom lawyer, helped advance his career perhaps more than anything else.

The final benefit that Clark realized as civil district attorney was made possible by those contacts that he made with judges. An oil boom for a man named Columbus Marion ("Dad") Joiner had caused legal problems for a great many people. While still a small and unsuccessful businessman, Joiner had divided his business into shares and sold these shares to hundreds of individuals to finance his oil exploration. Since Joiner was so unsuccessful, the shares seemed relatively worthless, and many shareholders didn't keep good track of them. Then Joiner suddenly hit oil—and the value of each share reached a remarkable $1,800. Since so many shares were in circulation, and since many additional ones had been forged as well, no one really knew who should get how much money. The courts were forced to settle the matter. The Dallas judge who received the case found that there was too much information for one individual to review, so he appointed Clark as a "special master" to assist the court in sorting out the facts of the case. For his time, energy, and expertise, Clark earned a substantial amount of money, enabling him to leave the civil district attorney's position and return to private practice.

Clark and his friend District Attorney Bill McCraw entered private practice together in 1932. McCraw, however, was not content to remain a private practitioner: he had the ambition of becoming the governor of Texas. In 1934, the office of attorney general of Texas was up for election. Since McCraw saw the position as a useful stepping stone to the governor's mansion, he decided to run.

Two other men, far more experienced and far better known, also were candidates for the office. However, McCraw traveled far and wide across the state of Texas, and he worked tirelessly for the job. He always had the help and support of his friend Tom Clark, who was his campaign manager. More than fifty years afterward, Clark's son Ramsey recalled McCraw and that election, and remembered how his father had toiled in the campaign. "Dad would work night and day," he said, "and in that pursuit, he was driving all across the state, trying to get Bill McCraw elected. . . . He fell asleep driving a car over in East Texas . . . and nearly killed himself and another person in the car."[3] With all the effort and energy behind his campaign, McCraw managed to win the election. Clark, after less than two years of private practice, was left without a partner.

It was not difficult for Clark to find a few young attorneys to hire. His law firm did well; being the friend and former partner of the new attorney general of the state did not go unnoticed, especially in a time in history when "machine" politics—politics in an area controlled by a political organization that may use dishonest means to do the controlling— was common and in which the social environment was also highly political. In fact, Clark went before committees of the state legislature on several occasions to answer questions about possible unethical involvement he might have had with Bill McCraw. Clark strongly denied any wrongdoing and believed that he was being victimized by McCraw's political enemies. No one was ever able to attach misconduct of any kind to Clark, then or in the future. Later in his career, as a high government official in the executive branch, Clark was approached with an offer to join a New York law firm with an annual salary worth perhaps as much as all the money he had ever earned as a lawyer. But money wasn't Clark's interest—as a young attorney in Dallas or a powerful official in Washington. He turned the law firm down.

The Clarks prospered financially during the "post-McCraw" period—and it cannot be linked just to the McCraw association, since McCraw was not reelected to his job as attorney general and never became governor. With the security of a comfortable living, Clark was able to think about moving beyond the walls of his Dallas office. As it did in his friend McCraw, the aspiration for public service also ran in Clark's veins. Unlike McCraw, however, Clark did not feel the urge to run for office; on the contrary, he wanted to serve as an executive in the Department of Justice. U.S. Senator Tom Connally, a longtime friend of the Clark family, acted as a sort of sponsor for Clark; in 1937, Connally announced that Clark had been chosen as an assistant attorney general of the United States. Without further delay, Clark packed up his wife and kids, closed his law office, and headed to Washington, D.C. When he arrived, it soon became clear that he had not been named assistant attorney general, but rather assistant *to* the attorney general—which is a very different job. The title "Assistant to the Attorney General" is simply an indirect way of saying "low level lawyer," someone who does routine legal work but doesn't make important policy decisions.

The discrepancy between Clark's expected job and the one he was actually offered may well have resulted from a political disagreement between President Roosevelt and Clark's patron, Senator Connally. But whatever its source, it provided Clark the first real dilemma of his career. What should he do? He and Mary pondered his options.

At the foreground of their minds was the possibility of immediately returning to Dallas and continuing the law practice. There remained in Texas all the family that the Clarks had; their friends were there; and they could count on a successful law career. However, Clark did not want to look like a fool or a quitter by running home at the first sign of trouble.

The other option was to stay in Washington and simply do the best he could. There was nothing dishonorable about being a government attorney at a troubled time for the country; in fact, it seemed the contrary. Although Clark's pride was certainly wounded, his previous struggles with money and his family showed that he was by nature a humble man who could accept what fate dealt. The plan of staying for a relatively brief time, serving the country, and then deciding whether to return home honorably if the family's prospects in Washington did not improve—or staying if they did— seemed a good one to the Clarks.

They decided to stay in Washington. It seems unlikely, judging by the rest of Clark's life, that it could have been any other way. A man unwilling to give in to poor circumstances, Clark often demonstrated the strong, tenacious streak in his nature.

At the same time that Tom Clark was a government employee, he was also a husband, father, and citizen. Although Clark has indeed been called a workaholic—even by his wife, Mary—he was also dedicated to his family and community during his years of service. When the family moved to Washington in 1937, their daughter Mimi was only four years old. Ramsey, their son, was not quite ten. Consequently, the children did not grow up in Texas as their parents did, although they definitely knew that they were from Texas and were proud of that. Mimi Clark Gronlund later wrote that her "romantic perception of the state was based on secondhand knowledge rather than actual experience."[4] This was significant not only about how the Clarks raised their children to be Texans but also about Tom Clark's own perception of himself as a Texan who was "temporarily out of state." The Clarks' residence in Washington was never supposed to become permanent; the planned return to Dallas was always a given.

* * *

Clark's new job was a routine one, but it would soon pick up momentum. In 1937, the Justice Department was still handling claims from World War I. It is impossible to say how long the judiciary and the Justice Department would have allowed these cases to sit, but fate entered into the situation and changed an ordinary job into one glistening with possibilities.

The year 1937 was one of the most unusual years in the history of the American court system. It was in this year, the first of Franklin Roosevelt's second term, that the president offered a plan to "pack the Supreme Court." Roosevelt had not yet been able to appoint a single justice to the Supreme Court, which was frustrating to him because every other president in history who served at least a full term had been able to appoint one or more justices during his years in office. The sitting court ("nine old men") invalidated plan after plan and act after act of the president's program for economic recovery and social reform, called the New Deal. It was disheartening for the president and his fellow New Dealers when the Court struck down even the cornerstone of Roosevelt's plan, the National Recovery Act. The president realized that the Court would not soon bend to meet his needs, so he decided to bend the Court.

In a plan he announced to the nation over the radio and then sent to Congress, Roosevelt suggested that the justices were too old to conduct their business; therefore, he said, any justice who reached the age of seventy and chose not to avail himself of the opportunity to retire with a pension would enable the president to appoint a second justice, to a maximum of fifteen members of the Court. In theory, these additional justices would help the Court with its workload.

Clearly, the problem was not that the justices could not do their work. One of Roosevelt's New Dealers recalled this premise years later in an interview, saying, "That was rubbish. It wasn't because they couldn't do their work. These old men were doing their work too damn well!"[5] No one was fooled into believing that President Roosevelt had any motive but political power behind his plan; specifically, he was determined to force the Court to support the New Deal. The public was opposed to Roosevelt's proposal, and so was Congress.

And new Assistant to the Attorney General Tom C. Clark was also opposed. He later recalled that he had been asked to lobby Senator Connally in favor of the president's plan but had refused to do so, perhaps as much as a matter of principle—being unwilling to serve as a political pawn for his superiors—as his own philosophical disagreement with it. Clark's superiors were apparently irritated at his refusal; he had no real work to do in his new job until the chief justice indirectly created some for him.

Ironically, Clark's resulting work came from the court-packing plan, the same policy that had placed Clark in the unpleasant situation of having nothing to do at the Justice Department in the first place. To prove that the judiciary was on top of its work, or perhaps to take Justice Department attention away from the court-packing plan, Chief Justice Hughes ordered the lower federal courts to clear out all claims from World War I. This would apply pressure to the executive branch, and as the attorney general's staff feverishly labored it would allow the courts to silently and ironically ask, Who can't do their work? Thus, Tom Clark's job was made a busy one by circumstances out of his control. Clark, the quintessential civil attorney, maintained his perfect record and never lost a single war-claims case. Things worked out well for Roosevelt too: the court-packing plan was abandoned after the Supreme Court began affirming Roosevelt's New Deal. In fact, from the day the president announced the plan, not a single piece of New Deal legislation was invalidated.

When the position of attorney general became vacant in 1939 upon the retirement of Homer S. Cummings, lawyers in the normally silent hallways of the Justice Department began choosing sides. One strong contender for the top job was a senior official in the department named Joseph Keenan. Apparently a great admirer of Keenan's, Tom Clark fervently supported him for the position of attorney general. But the ultimate decision, of course, belonged to President Roosevelt, who chose former Michigan Governor Frank Murphy for the job, despite a strong demonstration by many on Keenan's behalf. While Clark did not end up having a friend as attorney general, he did have a friend in Keenan in a position nearly as important: assistant attorney general. As a reward for Clark's support, Keenan arranged to place Clark in whatever section of the department he wanted, and Clark chose the antitrust section.

The well-known Thurman Arnold was assistant attorney general for antitrust at the time. An astute observer of political and legal skill and ability, Arnold saw talent in Clark that he wanted to tap and began placing Clark in job after job throughout the United States that would enable the antitrust section to benefit from Clark's ability. One of the first assignments Clark received was to go to New Orleans, Louisiana, to wrap up some antitrust business there. He remained for six months, while Mary went to Dallas during his absence. When the Clarks returned to Washington, a surprise was in store for them: Arnold had decided that Clark should head the section's West Coast office.

Thus, in 1940, the Clarks headed off to California. As soon as he got there, Clark handled a case in sixty days that an entire staff of lawyers and secretaries had spent two years trying to settle. Arnold's confidence in Clark was well founded.

Less than two years later, the Japanese attacked the United States at Pearl Harbor, Hawaii. This led to a near-hysterical anti-Japan scare among the American people, particularly in California. One congressman, John Rankin, voiced his opinion to other lawmakers in February 1942: "I'm for catching every Japanese in America, Alaska, and Hawaii now and putting them in concentration camps. . . . Damn them! Let's get rid of them now!"[6] Responding to the public frenzy, the president established the Western Defense Command and soon appointed Clark as its "civilian coordinator." By March of 1942, Japanese-Americans, who were U.S. citizens, were being transported to relocation centers—camps where they were forced to live—in western states. Their property was often sold at ridiculously low prices, since they could not take it with them; their new living quarters were often less than ideal; and ironically, while their families were in confinement centers under suspicion of being traitors, some twenty-five thousand Japanese-Americans served in the U.S. armed forces.

Clark was the liaison between the military and the government, focusing on legal action necessary to maintain security against the Japanese. The ultimate job that Clark had was to be the legal representative and enforcer of the program designed to move Japanese-Americans into camps located in inland America, to protect the country from possible subversion. He later described himself as the "'go-between' with the public" for General John DeWitt, the military head of the Western Defense Command.[7]

Eleanor Roosevelt was not the only person who abhorred the placement of free Americans in forced camps, but the majority of the people, giving in to their fears, agreed with the president that such actions should be taken in order to protect American security. (Not a single Japanese-American has ever been proven to have been disloyal to the United States.) The decision to isolate the citizens was made by the leaders of the executive branch. Tom Clark, as a Justice

Department attorney, merely was following orders, but he later claimed that his participation in the Japanese relocation effort was "the biggest mistake of my life" and a mistake he was willing to admit publicly.[8] Regretting the relocation program, Clark said that "a free society judges by individual acts, not by ancestry.... . Indeed, the Department of Justice successfully handled a similar problem involving persons of Italian and German extraction, dealing with them on an individual basis rather than by mass incarceration."[9]

Congress later formally apologized and offered monetary compensation to victims of the relocation program. While the program is now seen as both unforgivable and unacceptable, Tom Clark helped keep this horror from turning savage or brutal. In trying to guarantee livable conditions and the safety of the Japanese-Americans, Clark risked his own life: he was almost shot, for example, by an angry mob in Colorado who did not want a camp in their area.

The case of *Korematsu v. United States* tested the legality of the program in the Supreme Court. Writing for the majority of six justices in 1944, Justice Hugo Black declared that government had the power in times of war to take steps that would be unthinkable in peacetime. The ability to round up Japanese-Americans, he said, was included in this power.

* * *

After his job on the West Coast had been concluded, Clark was recalled to Washington—and there he lived until his death in 1977. Upon returning to the Justice Department, Clark was placed (within the antitrust section) in charge of the War Frauds Unit. It was in that position, prosecuting those suspected of trying to make personal gains through the government's war spending, that Clark made one of the most important friendships of his life. Heading a U.S. Senate committee also investigating war frauds was Senator Harry Truman from Missouri. Because investigative work threw them together, Clark and Truman got to know each other very well and became friends.

Clark's career took an upswing in 1943 when Thurman Arnold became a federal appeals court judge. Finally taking the position he thought he had been given in 1937, Clark was made assistant attorney general for antitrust, filling the position vacated by his friend Arnold. A new attorney general, Francis Biddle, reorganized the Justice Department in 1944, placing many of the duties of the antitrust division in the criminal section. Clark moved along with this change. He became the assistant attorney general in charge of criminal prosecutions, a highly coveted position.

Later that year, national politics began playing a larger role in Clark's life. The 1944 Democratic National Convention was determined to replace Vice President Henry Wallace—but with whom? At the convention, both Senator Truman and Clark supported Texas's favorite son, House Speaker Sam Rayburn. However, much as he would have liked to have been vice president, Rayburn could not attend the convention due to internal trouble in the party back in Texas. Thus, his momentum died and it became clear that he would not receive the nomination of the delegates. Harry Truman himself became a leading candidate, and midway through the convention, the president sent word to the delegates that he would be happy with either Supreme Court Justice William O. Douglas or Truman as the vice presidential nominee. Eventually, Truman, with Clark's strong support, won out, and when President Roosevelt died in April of the next year, Truman became president of the United States. His friend and supporter Tom C. Clark would greatly benefit from his association with the new president.

CHAPTER TWO

ATTORNEY GENERAL
AND THE COLD WAR

President Truman became famous for appointing friends and supporters to high positions. While Tom Clark clearly fit this category, Truman knew that Clark had bona fide credentials to serve as attorney general of the United States. First, he was a career lawyer in the Justice Department who knew how the organization was run and who could maintain stability during a difficult era; second, he was an able administrator who could also communicate well with his boss, the president; and finally, he had the strong backing of the powerful Texas delegation in the Congress, support that Truman would find necessary and useful during his administration. For these reasons, Truman chose Clark as his attorney general.

The timing was just right for such a move. During his years in the Justice Department, Clark always had planned to return to Dallas after his service in Washington came to an end. Apparently, Clark decided that his goal in the capital was to earn the office he thought he had been given to start with—assistant attorney general. By 1945 he had already served as assistant attorney general in two divisions—

antitrust and criminal prosecutions. Having accomplished his goal, the Clarks anticipated moving back to Texas.

They did move that year—but it was to an apartment in the middle of Washington, D.C. The dramatic change in plans was due to a strange twist of fate that would forever change the lives of the Clarks and their children. The sudden death of President Franklin D. Roosevelt was unexpected, and the Clarks knew that Tom had achieved as much as he could hope to under him. But when Harry Truman entered the White House, a whole new dynamic was inserted into the Clarks' plans. Not only was there still room for professional growth in national government, but Tom was given the opportunity to work among and be part of the most powerful group of people in the world as well. They would never leave Washington or their apartment again; in fact, Mary still lives there today.

Clark proved to be popular within the Department of Justice. While the office of attorney general usually went to highly qualified people, they had always previously been politicians, famous lawyers, or friends of the president. Tom Clark was the first "career lawyer" to reach the top job, a feat that must have engendered feelings of hope and optimism among the department's junior members. The new attorney general decided to have his swearing in at the Justice Department, so that all could attend, instead of a more elite ceremony at the White House, as previous attorneys general had preferred. He established open-door policies and other innovations that earned the support of his subordinates, for he was clearly down to earth and willing to focus on business rather than protocol.

Years later, looking back on his career, he noted that the attorney general's "office appointments come about every 15 minutes all day and into the night," which must have been exhausting to him.[1] Life was busy for the Clarks during the four years Tom headed the Department of Justice. Working at a frenetic pace, in charge of thousands of employees,

*The Clark family celebrates Clark's appointment to be
Attorney General: (left to right) Ramsey Clark, Mimi Clark,
Tom Clark, Mary Clark, 1945.*
FROM THE TOM C. CLARK PAPERS, TARLTON LAW LIBRARY,
UNIVERSITY OF TEXAS AT AUSTIN

dealing with and advising the president on the most sensitive and critical national issues, Clark was hard-pressed to
find extra minutes in a day. And, largely because he knew
what it felt like to be a Justice Department lawyer at a low
level, his efforts to maintain a feeling of openness in the
department made him perhaps the most accessible attorney
general up to that time in American history.

Despite this, Clark was able to function as a husband
and father. One thing in his favor was that there were no
small children to nurture as he entered the upper echelons

of government. His son Ramsey was old enough to leave home by that time, and the Clarks had only their daughter Mimi still living with them. She went through high school with her father serving as the nation's highest law enforcer and, later, one of the nation's highest judges.

Equally important was the excellent relationship he had with his wife. He called her "the beautiful mother" and loved spending time with her. Mary Clark was seen as "the vivacious member of the family . . . a constantly bubbling southern lady with a Texas accent, a remarkable talent for names, and a warmth of personality that makes her a favorite among Washington hostesses."[2]

The new attorney general entered office at an unusual period: the transition between World War II and another war, a war of words and threats that would come to be known as the Cold War. Like most other wars, the Cold War was fought over the conflict of ideas between two powers. These ideas were not just abstract principles but were articulated and executed by individuals on both sides—the United States and the Soviet Union—who had specific roles, agendas, and functions in their respective governments.

Because the Cold War was a war of ideas, the American government was forced to fight it on two fronts: internationally, as the government opposed the spread of Communism abroad, and internally, as it opposed the spread of Communist ideas and objectives among the people of the United States. Harry Truman, as the first Cold War president, was significant in establishing precedent for the American positions that would be followed throughout the duration of the war. Much of his policy was developed and carried out by the Department of Justice, the legal arm of the president. For this reason, Tom C. Clark, as the first Cold War attorney general, was an important figure of the era. His years of government service coincided with the early stages of the Cold War. Clark, as an American Cold Warrior, was an extremely influential official who personally clarified and defended

Attorney General Tom C. Clark, 1945.
FROM THE TOM C. CLARK PAPERS, TARLTON LAW LIBRARY,
UNIVERSITY OF TEXAS AT AUSTIN

much of the policy of the United States on internal affairs relating to the war.

Truman named Clark to be attorney general in late May 1945. By this point in World War II America and the Allies had achieved their goals of ending Hitler's domination of Europe, but the war was still raging in the Pacific. Atomic bombs were not dropped on Japan until more than two months after Clark began his term of office. The time following the conclusion of World War II was a difficult one; although Americans were jubilant at their success, international concerns loomed on the horizon. Tensions between the United States and the Soviet Union were increasing rapidly because the diplomacy that held them together during the war no longer existed. Additionally, new, serious issues had been created between the two countries: the fate of the European countries that had been conquered during the war, the future of Poland and Germany, and international postwar economic development. More than these, however, the issue of atomic energy—and who should be privy to the secrets of nuclear power—separated the United States and Russia.

These issues only indirectly concerned Tom Clark in his capacity as attorney general. But such related problems as national security and the need for loyalty in government devoured much of his time. Nevertheless, he would have preferred to have focused on such social problems as juvenile delinquency.

Late 1945 and 1946 were spent working out large international political problems. Governments were trying to use diplomacy to minimize their differences about how to resolve the dilemmas created by the war's end. At this point, it was unclear what the nature of U.S.-Soviet relations would be; if the two nations were to remain cordial and the problems mentioned above could be solved, later policies on loyalty and secrecy would be unnecessary.

In 1946 Winston Churchill made his famous statement about the "iron curtain" being created by Soviet takeovers in

Eastern Europe. These actions, coupled with Soviet resistance to American initiatives, led to fear on the part of the Truman administration of what President Ronald Reagan would later call an "evil empire."[3]

In March 1947 President Truman announced his famous Truman Doctrine, determined to help the governments of Greece and Turkey avoid ideological takeover by the communist Soviet Union. Not long afterward, Secretary of State George Marshall established his plan, similar to Truman's, promising economic aid to rebuild the war-torn European countries. But he also wanted to offer an opening to those countries that had already come under Soviet domination. These actions, which threatened the Soviet Union, as well as continuing conflict and fear over who should know the secrets of nuclear power, helped to further disintegrate U.S.-Soviet relations.

The reverberations from the international conflict were clearly felt back in the United States, where fears led to rising government awareness of Communists in America. They also caused Truman and Clark to begin searching for ways to make sure that Communists were not government employees. As early as September 1946, American Communists were accusing Clark of "red-baiting," or going out of his way to trap anyone with any possible sympathy for Communism, as well as of "seeing no difference between Communism and fascism."[4]

Over the next few months, however, Congress and the public increased pressure on the administration to oppose Communism more actively. The pressure was not entirely new: the House Committee on Un-American Activities had been formed in 1938, headed by another Texan, Representative Martin Dies Jr. The hostile atmosphere in Congress toward Communism in the late 1940s helped fuel the investigations of Wisconsin's Republican Senator Joseph McCarthy, which began in early 1950. Thus, even by early 1947, widespread discontent about the administration's anti-Communist policy was evident in Congress: many legislators felt that there *was* no coherent policy. Tom C. Clark, the attorney general and ostensibly the executive department official having the most influence in the internal war against subversive organizations, was particularly assailed. In April of 1947, New Jersey Representative Parnell Thomas "formally asked President Truman . . . to order Attorney General Tom C. Clark to prosecute Communists as 'criminal conspirators.'"[5] Thomas had tried, unsuccessfully, since October 1946 to obtain some abstract promise from Clark to crack down on Communist activities. Clark did not respond; instead, he wanted to wait for direction both from Truman and from the course of current events.

Soon enough, however, it became clear that tensions between the United States and the Soviet Union were making the conflict between capitalism and Communism ever more violent and more important. When the espionage of American citizens and foreigners in the United States who helped the Soviet Union obtain the secrets necessary for building the atomic bomb was exposed, the government's fear of subversives was to some extent justified.

In November 1947 President Truman, through an executive order, asked Attorney General Clark to prepare a list of organizations that were "totalitarian, fascist, Communist, or subversive" so that the government would have some guide to judge which groups were most likely to be disloyal. The presence of such a list did not change the fact that "guilt by association has never been one of the principles of our American jurisprudence. We must be satisfied that reasonable grounds exist for concluding that an individual is disloyal," as Attorney General Clark commented as he released the list.[6]

The list was one of Clark's ways to combat the spread of Communism in the United States. But Clark had wanted to do more than fight what already existed; he wanted to instill patriotism in Americans and remind them of what was good about their country to prevent future subversive behavior. For this reason, Clark had announced six months earlier, in May 1947, that he was establishing the "Freedom Train" to travel the country. The train carried to some two hundred cities over one hundred historical documents that had shaped American government.

Clark's concern about extensive subversive behavior, though not formally announced until the release of the attorney general's list, is evident in his comments inaugurating the Freedom Train. He claimed that there was "shocking evidence of disloyalty to our government," saying that "I feel that we have an appeal that can tug at the heartstrings of America, that can be the springboard of a great crusade for reawakening faith in America in the hearts of our people."[7] Clearly, Clark wanted to oppose Communism from two directions—attacking it from behind by exposing and suffocating it with the list of subversive organizations as well as meeting it head on by promoting patriotism and loyalty through the Freedom Train. If young people would learn and be excited by the roots and ideas of American government, he reasoned, they would probably be immune from Communist ideas.

Clark's years as attorney general, then, were largely devoted to the elimination of Communism—not in the international environment, with which most Cold Warriors are associated, but in the United States. However, this is not to imply that his tenure as attorney general was free from criticism. Some members of Congress were irritated by Clark's seemingly tardy response to the Communist "crisis" in America. Other individuals who were more interested in civil liberties criticized his list of subversive organizations; those who were placed on the list were especially vocal. Another problem with Congress came as a result of the Freedom Train.

A few months after Clark announced the creation of the Freedom Train, Michigan Republican Representative Clare Hoffman, chairman of the House Committee on Expenditures in the Executive Departments, made public a letter he had sent to Clark that essentially accused the administration of using the train for political purposes. Hoffman denied that Clark had any true interest in the patriotism of Americans, instead saying that it was "quite obviously just a build-up for 1948," pointing out that the train was scheduled to run until just two months before the presidential election of 1948.[8] No evidence has ever been presented of any intentions except the genuine desire to strengthen American postwar feeling about the United States, however, and the Freedom Train has generally been praised for its intentions.

Throughout the years that Clark served as attorney general, the government was developing and experimenting with its anti-Communism and proloyalty programs. Clark realized immediately that these "patriotic" intentions could turn into a test of political orthodoxy or—worse yet—tools for destruction of political opponents. This, of course, became the case with Senator McCarthy in the 1950s. In 1947, the administration was already concerned about the possibility of congressional investigations on the spread of Communism turning into "witch hunts" and at least indicated a fervent desire to avoid that. Clark and Truman both felt that the House Committee on Un-American Activities had stepped over the bounds of propriety, and they both criticized it as irresponsible, trying to exaggerate the extent of Communist infiltration to help its leaders in the political arena. Additionally, not only did Attorney General Clark, in announcing his famous list, make a special note that no one could be considered guilty by association (a promise congressional committees would later not be as eager to support), but he also made other statements designed to emphasize the same point. In a speech, appropriately at a "Jefferson Day Dinner," honoring the individual who had written the declaration announcing America's freedom from foreign tyranny, Clark declared that in his war on Communism Americans would be free from domestic tyranny. He said that "there will be no witch hunt, no whitewash, no raids, no third degree."[9]

Earlier in the month, an editorial in the *New York Times* had praised Clark's desire to keep the fight against Communism legal, ethical, and fair, saying that if "our loyalty program sticks to these principles it will never be abused. They are themselves a measure of loyalty."[10]

Although Clark had little to do with it, certain members of the government later would indeed abuse the principles he had established. The House Un-American Activities Committee and Senator McCarthy are particularly remembered for their roles in magnifying Communist involvement in government beyond reasonable proportions. McCarthy gave his name to "McCarthyism," a method of using smear tactics to destroy the credibility of accused Communists; some might even say that McCarthyism is synonymous with political repression. He was humiliated by a Senate reproof in 1954 (after both Truman and Clark had left the executive branch) for embarrassing the Senate through his actions, both on his own and in heading a Senate subcommittee. The House committee was known for calling witnesses who had to answer questions about their (and others') past involvement with groups that had been labeled as subversive. These congressional actions caused Clark to reenter the quagmire of internal Cold War issues in his next position: associate justice of the Supreme Court of the United States.

Clark had risen fast. The son of a Texas lawyer who had fallen on hard times, he rose to become the highest ranking lawyer in the United States. Even more, he was considered a good one by most who knew him or knew of him. A special award he received on May 29, 1946, is perhaps overly flattering but still accurate. The Texas State Society, in honoring the attorney general, said that the "man whom we are honoring tonight exemplifies the virtue, stability, and aggressiveness of those great men who in the past have lead [*sic*] the State of Texas to the enviable position it now occupies among the great states of the Union."[11]

CHAPTER THREE

INTO THE
MARBLE TEMPLE

Few people would be surprised to hear that many justices of the Supreme Court once served as attorney general. The nation's highest lawyer should, after all, be as well prepared as anyone else to serve as one of the nation's highest judges. Other reasons, besides being well qualified professionally, have influenced presidents to transfer someone from the Justice Department to the Supreme Court. In some cases, the president truly felt that the attorney general was the best man for the job. In others, however, it has been suggested that the attorney general was "kicked upstairs" because he was too honest, too uncompromising, or just not a good match with the president's style.

One former attorney general who became a Supreme Court Justice was Frank Murphy, the man who in 1939 had been appointed attorney general by President Roosevelt instead of Joseph Keenan, who had been supported by Clark. The next year, Murphy changed jobs once more when Roosevelt named him to the Supreme Court. But in 1949, Justice Murphy suddenly died, and President Truman was faced with a vacancy on the Supreme Court. Truman decided to place his own attorney general, Tom C. Clark, in the open seat.

Speculation varies as to Truman's reason for the promotion. It is most commonly believed that Clark was being rewarded for his service to the president during Truman's campaign and the four years he had served in office. John Frank wrote that, when Justice Murphy died, Truman immediately asked Clark to take the job, expressing not only satisfaction at Clark's work as attorney general but also the expectation that Clark could do a good job in the Court as well. A less frequently stated theory is that Clark pressed Truman hard for the job and won out by the force of bickering and by his strategic advantage in holding the office of attorney general, who traditionally suggests candidates for Court vacancies to the president. Clark later retold this story, in which he said, "I followed the practice of suggesting three names to the President when a judicial vacancy occurred, and my three choices when Justice Murphy died were Tom Clark, Tom C. Clark and Brother Clark, the President choosing the latter!"[1] The final possibility is that Truman wanted to get rid of Clark as an executive department official, but because it would have caused political trouble if he had tried to fire him, he moved Clark on to the next logical extension—and out of the cabinet.

Grains of truth may be found in all three theories. Certainly Truman and Clark were good friends, and Truman may have felt that he owed something to Clark for his unswerving support. It is not unlikely that Clark would have advanced his own interests. And Truman may well have been ready for a change in the Justice Department even if he was completely satisfied with Clark's performance. Even so, the first theory seems most in keeping with both Clark's and Truman's characters. Truman was known for giving his friends positions in government; this was, of course, a primary reason Clark became attorney general in the first place. Clark later noted that his move to the Supreme Court, thus vacating his position as attorney general, created a chain reaction in which several Truman friends were rewarded by the president with appointments to the vacant positions.[2] But it is extremely unlikely that Truman would have used one of his chief privileges of office, choosing Supreme Court justices, simply to create openings at lower levels for cronies. Clark, while a friend of Truman's, was also clearly qualified (although pundits said that Chief Justice Fred M. Vinson supported Clark "because he wanted someone on his Court who knew less law than he did"). Nevertheless, one researcher claims that "Clark is the most underrated Justice in recent Supreme Court history."[3]

Whatever the cause, the result was the same: the name of Thomas Campbell Clark of Texas was announced as Truman's nominee on July 28, 1949, and only three weeks later, on August 18, he was confirmed by the Senate after a somewhat rancorous debate. The confirmation process in the middle part of this century was nothing like it is today. For example, in 1939 Justice William O. Douglas was confirmed on the day he was nominated, a process quite different from the hours of testimony from judges like Clarence Thomas or Robert Bork, who have been nominated to the Supreme Court in recent years. The presence of the nominee before senators for questioning is itself a relatively recent invention.

In Clark's case, the process was lengthened from the standard of his day. Although the three weeks that the Senate spent in considering the president's nomination is short compared to the time spent today, it was unusual in 1949. Clark encountered some opposition from both ends of the political spectrum. Conservatives felt that Clark was no friend to states' rights and would be too liberal as a justice. Liberals, however, had their own specific objections. They pointed to Clark's part in the government's prosecution of Communists and claimed that he had no regard for the rights of individuals. Furthermore, they claimed that he was not friendly to civil rights cases and would be an obstacle to

31

progress on that front. Additionally, his positions in prosecuting crime as attorney general hardly had enamored him to those supporting an extension of the rights of criminal defendants. There was another and different concern as well. It had long been traditional that presidents honor the "Catholic seat" that Justice Murphy had occupied; that is to say, it was an unwritten rule to appoint a Catholic to fill that particular vacancy. However, Clark was a Presbyterian; this caused some resentment. Truman, of course, said that religion should not be a factor in choosing judges (but others pointed out that neither should personal friendship). In any event, the Senate finally voted 73–8 to confirm Clark.

The transition from lawyer to judge was magnified by the fact that Clark was not becoming merely a trial judge, whose work could be corrected by an appellate court. Rather, he was becoming a Supreme Court justice—a member of a small group whose work could be corrected by no one.

Most Supreme Court justices feel that the first few years on the Court are difficult, years spent in adaptation. When Clark joined the Court, he asked Justice Robert Jackson "how long it had taken him to get acclimated to the Court's work." When Jackson responded, he mentioned to Clark that he had asked Chief Justice Hughes the same question on coming to the bench, and had been told that it took three years. But Jackson told Clark that the truth was closer to five.[4] Like other justices, Clark also found the change challenging. Moving from the attorney general's office to the Supreme Court was not particularly easy for Clark. His daughter said that "the gregarious and energetic Tom Clark felt isolated and restricted" in the Supreme Court, which seemed "monastic compared to the frenetic pace of the attorney general's office."[5] When Clark served on the Court, each justice had a large office for himself, but only two additional rooms to house the justice's secretary, messenger, and his law clerks, of whom there were generally two. Moving from a position with countless staff members to having only four assistants was likely as difficult a transition as moving from the bustling, noisy, and crowded Justice Department to the silent halls of the Supreme Court.

Furthermore, President Truman placed him on the court as an ally, and his vote was expected to be one that would bolster the chief justice's, who was also a Truman appointee. At first, this seemed to be the case. Since Chief Justice Fred M. Vinson's philosophy was very similar to the moderate-conservative one that Clark possessed, it seemed only natural that Clark would agree in the majority of cases with Vinson. In the middle part of this century, the Supreme Court handed down between 150 and 225 full written opinions each year. In Clark's first term on the bench, he and Chief Justice Vinson disagreed on only two opinions—an unbelievable level of accord. Justices on the Court today are considered remarkably congruous in opinion if they agree on 75 percent of cases; no justices today agree 99 percent of the time as Clark and Vinson did.

As Clark spent more and more time on the Court, he developed more and more independence. Justices spend most of their time in the area of constitutional law, but Clark's experience was in antitrust and criminal law. Thus, as he learned more, he became more of an autonomous and authoritative voice on the Court.

* * *

The first major opinion in which Clark participated was the case of *Youngstown Sheet & Tube Co. v. Sawyer*. This landmark case is studied in many constitutional law classes today because it centered around the power of the president to take special actions in an emergency.

The country was in the middle of the Korean War in 1952, and President Truman felt that continuous production of steel was essential to the war effort. Every vital piece of military equipment required steel, and its absence would create chaos for the armed forces and would seriously threaten national security.

Perhaps the workers in the nation's steel mills realized their importance. Whether they were knowledgeable of their role in the war effort or not, they chose a strategic time to protest their wages and demand higher salaries. In late 1951 and early 1952, they officially went on strike, leaving the steel mills out of operation. President Truman was horrified, although he believed that their demand for better wages was reasonable. From his perspective, the problem was that the management of the mills refused to pay an increased wage. Truman decided that he would have to do something to stop the potential damage to the war effort.

Congress had written several laws designed to enable the president to act in an emergency of this kind. Prime among them was the Taft-Hartley Act of 1947, which, ironically, had been passed overriding Truman's veto. This law, recognizing the importance of certain industries for the American people, while balancing those interests with the right of the private sector to be free from unwarranted government intervention, allowed the president to call for mandatory talks between the owners and the workers of a plant and to postpone a strike for eighty days. Then the president would have to obtain the help of Congress in resolving any problems that still remained.

Neither the Taft-Hartley Act nor any other measure gave the president the authority to take control of the industry, a power that Congress had specifically voted down several years before the steel crisis erupted. Nevertheless, considering the grave national security problems involved, President Truman felt that he had no choice but to order the continued operation of the steel mills.

The president decided to issue an executive order. The order directed the Department of Commerce to take possession of the majority of the nation's steel mills and operate them. Upon receipt of the president's order, the secretary of commerce issued orders of his own that commanded federal possession of the mills. The managers of the mills were told to direct the operation.

Suit was filed in federal district court by the managers because they felt that the president had acted illegally; eminent domain was a congressional, not executive, power. They obeyed the order, but their suit progressed in the court system.

Meanwhile, the president had written to Congress explaining what he had done, asking for congressional help, and agreeing that Congress had the power to regulate his actions. Congress made no official negative or positive response; in fact, it did nothing. The U.S. District Court issued an injunction (a court order) prohibiting the president's order from going into effect, but an appeals court reversed the lower court. At that point, the Supreme Court accepted the case, and on May 12, 1952, it heard oral arguments.

Central to the president's argument was the idea of implied executive powers. As the commander-in-chief, the president would be expected to control anything in the "theater of war," even if that meant taking possession of private property.

However, Justice Hugo Black, writing for the Court, ruled that the president could not reasonably claim that as commander-in-chief he could extend his powers into the civilian arena to the extent that he did. The lawmakers of the country, the Court ruled, should establish rules for emergencies, which would be enforced by the president. Justice Clark agreed with this judgment.

The case is significant in Justice Clark's career because it marks his independence, as a judge, from President Truman, Chief Justice Vinson, or any other outside influence. In a brief concurring opinion, Clark wrote that, while "the Constitution does grant to the President extensive authority in times of grave and imperative national emergency," the president must still obey specific rules of Congress (such as how to resolve labor disputes) if "Congress has laid down specific procedures to deal with the type of crisis confronting the President." Simply stated, Clark would almost always have granted the president the power to deal with emergencies, and in this case he would do no less—he simply demanded that the laws of Congress be followed when they already covered a situation.

Three justices, including Vinson, dissented from the opinion of the Court. They claimed that, if the president is authorized by Congress to wage war, he is authorized by Congress to *win* the war. It only makes sense, Vinson reasoned, that the president would need steel to win the war and that he was implicitly granted the power to get the steel by the congressional authorization to conduct the war effort. Supporters of the president, in other words, might have suggested that removing Truman's right to obtain steel to fight the war was like asking a fireman to quench the flames of a burning house but denying him the use of water.

Truman, of course, was furious at the Court's decision. To him, the case was of as monstrous proportions as other notorious cases the Court had decided; he also saw the case as egregious judicial activism—judges substituting their own opinions for those of elected officials. But in a very real sense, Clark's opinion, concurring with the majority, was a model of judicial restraint. Clark bent over backward to recognize the power and authority of the president and in no way discussed his own opinion of the case. But he had other concerns: federal law established just what the president could and could not do. By strictly adhering to the law, Clark deferred to Congress and applied the law accordingly: Truman's desire, that the Court ignore the law and just give him the power to do what he wished, would arguably have been a much greater example of judicial activism than what the Court actually did.

Because Clark had been supportive of Truman's previous efforts to wield presidential authority when he was attorney general, Truman was surprised at his opinion. Furthermore, Truman had considered Clark a friend and ally. But *Youngstown* changed, perhaps fundamentally, this view. Clearly referring to this case, Truman said of Clark: "That damn fool from Texas that I first made Attorney General and then put on the Supreme Court. I don't know what got into me. He was no damn good as Attorney General, and on the Supreme Court . . . it doesn't seem possible, but he's been even worse. He hasn't made one right decision that I can think of. . . . It's just that he's such a dumb son of a bitch."[6]

Truman's words seem painfully harsh, but three comments may place them in a less bitter perspective. First, it should be recalled that Truman was never one to mince words; perhaps of all the presidents, he was the one most likely to be blunt and forthright, and to speak off the top of his head without considering his statements first. Second, Truman probably spoke in anger, and his words likely show more his resentment against the decision and his disappointment in not having the solid vote he expected than a personal dislike he developed for Tom Clark. Finally, the truth is that the two men remained friends until Truman died in 1972. They visited each other's homes and enjoyed each other's company, often playing poker together. Truman put Clark on the Court as an ally; while Clark's decisions were sometimes disappointing to Truman, Clark never stopped being a friend.

* * *

The *Youngstown* decision coincided historically with a greater transition. The year after it was handed down, Truman left office, succeeded by World War II hero Dwight D. Eisenhower. That year, Chief Justice Vinson died suddenly at the relatively young age of sixty-six, leaving a vacancy for President Eisenhower to fill. Eisenhower would later be disappointed in his choice for the nation's highest judicial

37

chair, but at the time he was widely congratulated on choosing California Governor Earl Warren. A fellow Republican, Warren had been helpful to Eisenhower in the election of 1952; many saw the appointment as a political payoff.

Whatever the politicians had expected of Earl Warren, they got an ideological reformer who leaned far more toward the liberal side of constitutional interpretation than the conservative approach favored by Chief Justice Vinson. Warren's sixteen years would cover one of the most turbulent eras in Supreme Court history. Tom Clark, seen by many as the cautious clone of Fred Vinson, and who was described after a year on the Court as a justice who "has shown an almost unbelievable unanimity of opinion with his Chief," would end up participating in some of the most important of the Warren Court decisions.[7]

But Clark seemed to be a restraining influence for the famously liberal and progressive Warren Court as well. This kind of influence can be accounted for by the fact that, although Justice Clark often supported the reforms instituted by Warren and the other liberal justices, he was hardly a member of a liberal "gang" that would go along with any liberal idea. Since there were often close votes, especially in the early years of Warren's tenure, every justice had significant power. Consequently, writing opinions that were palatable to as many members of the Court as possible was an important skill, and Clark's moderate leanings probably tilted the Warren Court back toward the center. If President Truman had appointed to the Court someone more liberal than Clark, constitutional law in the 1950s and 1960s may have ended up looking quite different from the way it appears today.

The first major case that the Supreme Court would decide under its new chief justice was one that had been postponed by the Vinson Court—because it fell in an election year. In an interview years later, United States Court of Appeals Judge Abner Mikva, who was at the time a law clerk for Justice Felix Frankfurter, recalled asking the justice why the case wouldn't be handed down in early 1952. He was shocked when Frankfurter responded: "You wouldn't expect us to hand down an important decision like this in an election year, would you?"[8] Frankfurter's objective was not itself political: he just wanted to stop politicians from tearing apart the case during an election season without having even understood it. Referring to this case and others like it, Justice Clark said in an interview much later that the justices "often delay adjudication. It's not a question of evading at all. . . . It's just the practicalities of life—common sense."[9]

The case, *Brown v. Board of Education*, had been scheduled to be decided in 1952, but the justices delayed the action because some of them, especially Justice Frankfurter, didn't want to decide it right before a presidential election. But why would that have been such a problem? The case was a controversial one, challenging longtime opinions about racial segregation. The standing rule was that blacks and whites could be segregated, or kept separate from each other, as long as their respective institutions (such as schools, parks, or transportation options) were "equal." Since racial issues were so emotional in America, the justices realized that, when they handed down a ruling to abolish segregation, a firestorm of controversy would erupt.

However, there is speculation that, had the case been decided in 1952 when Vinson was still chief justice, the results may have been quite different. It is clear from the notes Justice Robert Jackson took at conference, as well as other comments from various justices, that Chief Justice Vinson, Justice Stanley Reed, Justice Jackson, and Justice Clark were all inclined to let segregation stand as constitutional. All that would have been needed was a single vote from one of the other five justices—Harold Burton, William Douglas, Felix Frankfurter, Hugo Black, or Sherman Minton—and segregation could possibly be legal today.

However, there is equally strong evidence that the Court would have ruled in 1952 precisely the way it ended up ruling in 1954. Years later, Justice Clark stated that "the results would have been the same. . . . I don't see how any informed person could conclude to the contrary. Indeed, the result was forecast in *Sweat v. Painter,*" referring to a recent case that had weakened—but not destroyed—segregation.[10] Justice Clark did not have any doubt about the results; but this comment came twenty years after the fact.

His own record indicates opposition to racist practices in government; as attorney general, he took the unusual step of writing a "historic brief against racial covenants" that was presented to the Supreme Court in the case of *Shelley v. Kraemer.* The justices ruled that it was a violation of the Fourteenth Amendment for a court to enforce restrictive racial covenants, which amounted to contracts requiring landowners not to sell to African-Americans (or other non-whites). In the brief, Clark and Solicitor General Philip B. Perlman wrote that "segregation, rooted in ignorance, bigotry and prejudice, and nurtured by the opportunities it affords for monetary gains from the supposed beneficiaries and real victims alike, does exist because private racial restrictions are enforced by courts."[11] Clark asked the justices to end this practice, and Chief Justice Vinson, writing for the Court, did so. It would seem strange indeed for Clark and Vinson, paired up as lawyer and judge in opposition to government discrimination here, to team up in *Brown* to support it. Yet that is what some say would likely have happened had Vinson lived.

Nevertheless, there were never more than four justices ever considering supporting segregation, and no one can say for sure if they would truly have voted that way. There is enough evidence to show that none of the justices personally *liked* segregation and they actually thought that it was wrong; but justices cannot vote solely on their likes and dislikes, or even moral convictions. They must vote according to their understanding of the law of the Constitution, regardless of personal beliefs. So it was very possible that one or more justices would have voted for segregation, and although Justice Clark clearly denied it, some scholars think he might have been one of them. Even the possibility of a split vote is meaningful, because the eventual unanimous opinion was every bit as important for actually being unanimous as for being against segregation.

By the time the Supreme Court was ready to decide the case for the record, an important aspect of the Court's composition had changed dramatically. Vinson had been replaced by Warren, who quickly decided that segregation in public schools must not be allowed to stand.

First, the constitutional precedent, *Plessy v. Ferguson,* was based solely on the notion that the Fourteenth Amendment allowed facilities to be "separate but equal." *Plessy,* decided by the Supreme Court in 1896, came from Louisiana and was the result of a transportation problem similar to that experienced by Rosa Parks in 1955. Parks had boarded a Montgomery, Alabama, bus and sat in the "colored" section—the seats reserved for black people. But when enough whites boarded the bus, she was ordered to give up even that seat and was arrested when she refused. More than half a century earlier, Homer Plessy, who was one-eighth black, was forced off the area of a train reserved for whites only. Unlike in Rosa Parks's incident, from which a great movement for civil rights sprang up, Plessy's case resulted in the Supreme Court's deciding that states did not have to stop segregation and that segregation was not necessarily admission that one race was superior to another. The Court felt that, as long as the rule of "separate but equal" was observed, no one was denied a constitutional right. In the *Brown* ruling, Warren discarded this paradox: "the doctrine of 'separate but equal' has no place. Separate educational facilities are inherently unequal."

41

Second, the Warren Court discussed at length the social products of segregation, an aspect of the case heavily emphasized by Thurgood Marshall, an attorney with the National Association for the Advancement of Colored People (NAACP) who represented the family of Linda Brown, a student not wanting to attend segregated schools. This case was specifically about education: Topeka, Kansas, like many school districts, provided separate schools and facilities for children of different races. Beyond potential inequities in quality of instruction or resources, there were questions about the emotional and social ramifications of segregating young school children. Warren, in agreement with Marshall, decried the harm to self-esteem that could result from being separated solely on the basis of race. While some critics would later claim that this psychological spin was out of place in a court of law, others praised the pragmatic and realistic approach that tried to understand the needs and feelings of black Americans.

The opinion of the Court was unanimous, decided 9–0. Years later, a law clerk for Justice Reed, the justice most likely to uphold segregation, wrote that, although Reed believed he would have been joined by other justices had Vinson still been chief justice, by the time the case was reargued with Warren as chief, he felt that he was the only member of the Court who would vote against desegregation.[12] Earl Warren received most of the credit for the civil rights victory, and he deserved the accolades. Reed's comments notwithstanding, the unanimity of the opinion was reached only after hours and hours of lobbying, researching, and other difficult work on Warren's part.

But years later, in his memoirs, Warren said that he thought that most of the praise should be given to Justice Clark and the two other southern justices, Reed of Kentucky and Black of Alabama, because they had the most to lose. He pointed out that the justices from the South would face much more pressure and be subject to far more anger than those from the North. Warren, for example, was from California; there had been no history of legally mandated segregation there, so *Brown* would not cause the Californians to change their way of life too much. Consequently, the six justices who did not come from the South "were not in danger of being faced with animosity and harassment in [their] home states because of centuries-old patterns of life."[13] Clark exhibited a significant amount of courage in this case by concluding that his probable original position—that segregation was legal—was in error and then by turning away from an aspect of his southern heritage to join an opinion that he thought was right.

This certainly does not mean that Clark wanted to deny his Texas roots. The notable affinity Justice Clark and his family had for Texas did not change when he donned his judicial robes; in fact, love for Texas is one of Clark's most consistent characteristics. Clark's daughter cites a habit of her father as proof of his state pride. When she would bring friends home, he would often tell them that "they were 'pretty enough to be a Texan.'"[14] In her thesis, written in 1984 about her father's early life, she wrote:

> Being a Texan was special. I felt a surge of pride when I responded "Texas" to the familiar question "And where are you from?"—never doubting that everyone shared my lofty esteem of the state. "Mimi looks like a Texan," my father would declare, and I would beam, understanding the significance of the compliment. . . . Tom Clark was a Texan and remained one, although he lived more than half his life outside his native state. Even his physical appearance, aided by the Stetson hats and jaunty bow ties he loved to wear, fit the popular image of how a Texan should look. . . . Tom Clark's Texas heritage was more than physical, however. He reflected a Texas before the oil boom of the thirties brought the enormous wealth and gaudy materialism later associated with the state.[15]

43

His daughter was not the only one to notice Tom Clark's Texas flair; apparently, everyone noticed it. Legal scholar Bernard Schwartz wrote that "Clark continued to flaunt his Texas background" after he entered the Supreme Court. Schwartz noted that Clark and the other justices joked about it, as when Clark wrote to Chief Justice Warren that "the duck was delicious. . . . It was big enough to be from Texas" or when Justice John Marshall Harlan II wrote Clark a postcard about Australian farming, saying that "some of their sheep stations are nearly the size of the Sovereign State of Texas." Clark's pride in his state extended even into his work on the Court; in one case, he thought that his fellow justices were being unfair to Texas and almost dissented from the ruling.[16]

The love Clark bore for his state is obvious, as is the ease with which he transmitted it to his children. Both Ramsey and Mimi would later live in Dallas, although eventually they would return to the east. His fondness for his home state did not lead, however, to his advocacy of a racist past: as a Supreme Court justice, he hoped that he could make Texas and the United States better by using the Constitution to improve the rights of all Texans and Americans regardless of color.

The struggle that the Supreme Court conducted with civil rights was far from over with *Brown*, however. In 1958, the Court heard the case of *Cooper v. Aaron*. This case resulted from a phrase in the second *Brown* ruling that was being misapplied by southern states. The first *Brown* ruling, in 1954, had overturned the doctrine of "separate but equal" but had not addressed the specifics of educational segregation. Therefore, the Court heard arguments again and released its second—and also unanimous—opinion in *Brown* in 1955. In this second *Brown* ruling, the states had been told to desegregate "with all deliberate speed." This ambiguous term had been intended to indicate the Court's understanding that the educational systems of many states could not be changed instantly; what was expected was simply that the states would begin the process of change as rapidly as they could. But the phrase had the unfortunate effect of leading southerners to believe that the Court would allow them to stall indefinitely on implementing a new system of education, as long as they said that they were moving "with all deliberate speed."

In Louisiana, for example, the state refused to integrate and actually continued to build segregated schools. The state's rationale, simply, was that the people were not ready for such a violent change in so little time. The approach of the state, in theory, was to move incrementally toward the "goal" of desegregation and reach that goal when the public was "ready." Clearly, this caused conflict. Southern blacks believed that they had been given the right to desegregated schools by the Supreme Court and felt that the state's attempt to block this integration violated the Court's order. Finally *Cooper*, a case from Arkansas, came before the Court, with the school board—fully supported by the governor of the state—asking for permission to delay its implementation of the *Brown* ruling until it was feasible. The case was much publicized; at one point in 1957 President Eisenhower deployed federal troops to enforce a court order to allow black students to attend school with white students at Little Rock's Central High School.

The justices realized that their decision in *Brown* had been flawed because of the "deliberate speed" provision. To send a unified and clear message to the nation that purposeful delay, without the intention of complying with the order, was absolutely unacceptable, the nine members of the Court gathered around the conference table in the Supreme Court building. Together, they wrote the decision that was handed down. In past historic cases, such as *Brown*, the chief justice had written the opinion and delivered it in open court; in *Cooper*, all of the justices wrote the opinion and presented it together. Never before nor since in this century have all the members of the Court authored an opinion in unison.

Again, Justice Clark was a large part of the process. As one of the Court's most visible southern members, pressure was great on him to dissent. Throughout the nation, and particularly the South, people did not think that delay was particularly unreasonable, especially considering the massive and emotional change that the desegregation rulings would bring. Clark likely felt pressured to vote to grant a reasonable delay. His refusal to do so, and his willingness to help and join with all of his colleagues in sending the clearest of messages that segregation must stop immediately, speaks volumes about his character.

A case decided unanimously naturally carries greater weight with the public than does a split decision. When the nine most respected judges in the land all agree, it is generally conceded that they must be right. But if almost half the members of the Court dissent, people naturally feel less secure with the decision, since a change in the opinion of only one justice would have reversed the outcome. Each justice carries a tremendous amount of power; even a single dissent significantly decreases the weight of the decision. Had Clark refused to sign the opinion, or had he gone further and dissented, the clear and unified message that the Supreme Court wanted to send would have been lost.

Justice Clark would become one of the Court's foremost spokesmen on the subject of civil rights a few years later, but his votes in *Brown* and *Cooper* were historic in and of themselves. Those who appreciate the Supreme Court's positive role in improving racial equality owe a large debt of thanks to Justice Clark.

While the Supreme Court was dealing with the civil rights of black Americans it had to consider other important concerns as well. As attorney general, Clark had spent a great deal of time and energy working on ways to promote loyalty and detect subversive activity. His experiences in the Justice Department gave him strong feelings about the powers necessary for government to protect itself; not surprisingly, as a justice he seemed inclined to give the government the bene-fit of the doubt in anticommunist cases. Some of Justice Clark's most famous opinions center around the loyalty issues that were presented throughout his tenure. Although on some issues Clark was liberal, or at least less conserva-tive, he never lost his conservative point of view on cases where loyalty was the central question. Historian Richard Kirkendall, writing about Justice Clark's career, took a less charitable attitude toward Clark's proloyalty sentiments, saying that the former attorney general "brought the fears of the Cold War to the Supreme Court and helped to translate them into the law of the land."[17]

The first major case that he is known for is *Jencks v. United States.* Clark gained fame for his opinion in this case not because it became the law of the land but because it was a dissenting opinion. The Court's majority had ruled that, in a case involving an individual accused of subversive activi-ties, the defendant must be allowed access to government documents related to the issue. This included confidential documents in some of the nation's secret agencies, such as the FBI or the CIA. Justice Clark, recognizing the danger of such an action, issued a sharp dissent, in what was "for a mild-mannered man . . . an unusually intemperate fashion."[18]

In his dissent, Clark berated his brethren for ignoring precedent and taking phrases from prior opinions out of context. Clark was infuriated that the Court would go so far as to allow defense lawyers and accused criminals, instead of only the judges, to see confidential memos and other important documents. He wrote that, "unless the Congress changes the rule announced by the Court today, those intel-ligence agencies of our Government engaged in law enforce-ment may as well close up shop."

The Congress eventually did create the Jencks Act, which tightened security and removed some of the docu-ments in question from the domain of the papers that

*Justice and Mrs. Clark (seated) celebrate their 40th wedding
anniversary at the Supreme Court with (left to right)
son Ramsey Clark, daughter-in-law Georgia Clark, daughter
Mimi Clark Gronlund, and son-in-law Tom Gronlund, 1964.*
FROM THE TOM C. CLARK PAPERS, TARLTON LAW LIBRARY,
UNIVERSITY OF TEXAS AT AUSTIN

defense lawyers could see. However, the statute was more in
response to the dissent in the case than to the majority
opinion. Critics of Justice Clark believed that he was exag-
gerating the scope of *Jencks;* perhaps his statement in the
dissent that "the Court has . . . afforded [the criminal] a
Roman holiday for rummaging through confidential information as well as vital national secrets" was overly sensational.
What Clark thought so unbelievably ironic in this situation
was that people accused of trying to subvert the government

were granted a significant amount of access to the exact information that the government was trying to protect! It made no sense to Clark that accused spies should be given a key to the CIA.

With such interesting and important issues coming before him on a daily basis, it must have been difficult for Clark not to have talked about them once he got home. Yet he always interacted with his family as a *family,* neither discussing the legal problems he faced when attorney general nor the cases that came before him after he became a Supreme Court justice. It wasn't only that it would have been improper to discuss highly sensitive and confidential information with those not privy to government secrets. It was also that, when he was home, Clark was a doting father who enjoyed spending time with his children and buying them presents. He preferred to play with his family rather than talk about law with them. His chances for relaxing family time had to be savored. Throughout his years in Washington, Clark would often work late but would come home and spend time with his wife and children. After dinner and conversation he would frequently stay up until Mary went to bed, and then he would go to his study and work several more hours.

* * *

Back at the Court, Clark had new cases, and occasionally variations on old ones. For example, similar in nature to the *Jencks* decision was the case of *Watkins v. United States.* In this case, a man was convicted of contempt of Congress for refusing to divulge the names of certain individuals who had at one point been members of the Communist Party in America (but who no longer were) to the House Un-American Activities Committee. Watkins, the defendant, claimed that such a statement would not only be on his part pointless and contrary to the needs of Congress but that it would also

49

deprive those individuals (who had "mended their ways") of their own rights. For refusing to give this information, which the committee deemed essential, Watkins was convicted.

When the case came to the Supreme Court, Chief Justice Earl Warren wrote the majority opinion; Justice Clark was alone in dissent. The majority held that Congress may certainly conduct investigations but may not deprive witnesses of any of the liberties that they might face in a courtroom. One such right might be the freedom from questions that do not pertain to the case or controversy at hand. Hence, considering the lack of understanding of the purpose of certain questions given to Watkins—such as those concerning the identities of former Communists—the Court held the conviction invalid.

Clark was less passionate in his dissent here than he had been in *Jencks*. He first disagreed with the majority's demand that Congress restrict the questions it could ask witnesses to those questions that would be admissible in a court of law. Clark claimed that Congress could ask witnesses anything it wanted to, with only two conditions. First, he said, the subject that a congressional committee wanted to investigate must be a legitimate object of legislative interest. Second, the question itself must be pertinent, or relating to, the subject of the investigation. The majority, in the name of "fair play," declared that the procedural rules that a court followed were now also applicable to Congress, but Clark rejected the imposition of these rules. The Supreme Court, he said, was not equipped to handle the functions of the other two branches of government. In other words, Clark felt that, within wide boundaries, Congress should be free to go about its business as it thought best, without having to worry about interference from the Supreme Court.

Finally, Justice Clark analyzed the merits of Watkins's case. He summarized the majority as reversing Watkins's conviction on account of, first, the lack of clarity of subject matter and, second, the lack of protection for constitutional rights employed by the structure of committee hearings. Clark denied both claims of the majority.

The subject matter of the investigation, Clark said, was crystal clear to Watkins—and also to Clark. "I think the Committee here was acting entirely within its scope and that the purpose of its inquiry was set out with 'indisputable clarity,'" he wrote in his dissent. Clark quoted from the committee chairman's statements and Watkins's own comments before the committee, as well as past investigations, to prove that the information that was needed was specific and available to Watkins; his refusal to answer, then, could not be justified by a claim of not understanding the theme of the hearings.

Clark then turned to the idea of the protection of constitutional rights. He dismantled the majority's assertion that the committee somehow would violate a witness's First Amendment rights. Clark said that the First Amendment protected Watkins's right to join and speak freely on behalf of any organization that did not wish to incite crime. But Watkins was trying to protect his friends, not himself—and Clark reminded the Court of a long-established canon of constitutional law, "that one cannot invoke the constitutional rights of another."[19]

Clark then used what to many people may seem like common sense. The First Amendment, he said, allows people to say what they want to; it does not allow them a right to be silent or to choose all the occasions in which they will speak.

Lucid as his arguments may seem, they did not attract the vote of even one other member of the Supreme Court. However, Clark was given an opportunity several years later to whittle down the *Watkins* decision. The cases of *Barenblatt v. United States* and *Uphaus v. Wyman,* which were handed down on the same day, enabled Justice Clark to speak with a new majority of justices who wished to back away from the precedent that they had set in *Watkins.*

Members of the Court, 1963. Standing (left to right) Justices Byron R.
White, William J. Brennan, Jr., Potter Stewart, Arthur J. Goldberg.
Seated (left to right) Justices Tom C. Clark, Hugo L. Black,
Chief Justice Earl Warren, Justice William O. Douglas.
Not pictured: Justice John Marshall Harlan II.
(Lonnie Wilson, *Oakland Tribune* Photo)
FROM THE TOM C. CLARK PAPERS, TARLTON LAW LIBRARY,
UNIVERSITY OF TEXAS AT AUSTIN

The Court came to a largely different conclusion in these
cases only two years after *Watkins* was decided. It is unusual
for the Supreme Court to come close to reversing itself so soon
after a decision has been announced. The doctrine of stare
decisis states that the Court will stand by previous decisions
unless there is a significantly grave constitutional reason to
overturn precedent. Sometimes justices who dissented in the
original ruling will support that ruling in later cases, even
though they originally disagreed with it, in order to follow stare

decisis. But in these cases, Clark maintained his original position and was joined by two justices who had opposed him in *Watkins* (Felix Frankfurter and John Marshall Harlan II, both considered conservative members of the Court) and by two justices who had not participated in the previous case (Potter Stewart and Charles E. Whittaker). This majority established some new guidelines for investigations by government agencies regarding membership in Communist organizations.

The *Barenblatt* case, written by Justice Harlan, was a simple one. A professor at the University of Michigan had been questioned by the same congressional committee as in *Watkins* and had refused to answer questions about his own involvement with Communists or about certain activities under the sponsorship of the Party taking place on campus. The Court affirmed his conviction.

In *Uphaus,* Clark wrote for the majority and acknowledged the power of the executive branch to conduct anticommunist investigations as well. The attorney general of New Hampshire had been given the authority to demand lists of guests at places where subversive activities might take place; the Court affirmed his ability to serve as a "one man legislative investigating body."[20] Clark noted that *Uphaus* concerned more than technical questions about governmental structure: the right that people had to interact privately with others and with groups, without fear of government scrutiny, was at stake. But, he wrote, "the governmental interest in self-preservation is sufficiently compelling to subordinate the interest in associational privacy of persons" who joined organizations that had been identified as subversive or whose mission was to advance Communist ideology. The Supreme Court, through Justices Clark and Harlan, gave a strong show of support to all levels of government wanting to ferret out subversives.

For the rest of his tenure on the Court, Clark maintained his conservative views on the threat of Communism and recognized the power of government to curb this threat. Not only did he support the government, but he was usually able to garner a majority to affirm his views.

Loyalty cases seemed to be predictable for Justice Clark. Starting in 1961, though, Clark began receiving a number of cases that were related more to civil liberties and civil rights; his decisions on these issues show an evolving philosophy of justice. Some of the most important opinions of the 1960s were written by Justice Clark; these opinions remain today as some of the bastions of modern law.

CHAPTER FOUR

GUARDING
CIVIL LIBERTIES

Certain times of the year were busier for Clark than others. The Supreme Court takes a summer break; the Court usually recesses in June, while the beginning of the Court's term is the first Monday in October. This gives justices the whole summer to work on their writing, to travel, to teach in law schools, or just to relax at home. But there is rarely a day, even in the summer, when something relating to the Court does not come up.

The Clarks enjoyed making brief trips. Occasionally, Justice and Mrs. Clark would go abroad with other members of the Court, especially the chief justice, to attend functions relating to the Supreme Court or the judiciary. The Clarks were able to travel or spend time leisurely more frequently than ever before. Before Clark joined the Court, trips were rare but cherished. Mrs. Clark today recalls how much she and her husband enjoyed short trips or vacations even when he was a junior member of the Justice Department.[1]

In addition to traveling, Clark worked at improving the American system of law. In the late 1950s Clark began expending significant energy as the chair of the American

Bar Association's Section of Judicial Administration. This was one of the first major positions in leadership that Clark accepted, and perhaps the one that ultimately led him, after retirement, to a position of eminence in the field of judicial reform. When he accepted the job, the section was not a significant force in the judiciary; in fact, only five hundred members belonged when Clark took over. After he made his mark, however, the section claimed over seven thousand. The group was a think tank of sorts that deliberated the administration of all the different courts—from the lowest to the highest. It was on such ventures, as well as traveling, writing, and reviewing Court documents, that Clark spent his summers and extra time.

When October came the justices all returned to Washington from wherever they had passed the summer. Whatever else each one may have expected about the upcoming year, they probably all felt sure that it would in some way make history. The Warren Court era brought more changes in constitutional law than any other period in Court history. The majority of these changes resulted from rules that the Court handed down relating to the rights of the individual—civil liberties.

The Bill of Rights was established in the United States as an afterthought. When the fifty-five framers of the Constitution met in Philadelphia in the summer of 1787, they chose not to include any specific protection for speech, religion, the press, or other important freedoms. The Constitution was a structural framework that set the government itself into motion. Many of the authors of the Constitution believed that, had they granted protection to the people for a specific right, all *other* rights could be infringed—in other words, listing certain rights might imply that no other rights were guaranteed. Since few wanted a government like that, they felt it best to leave out any mention of civil liberties and aim for the broadest measure of protection possible.

People who strongly favored states' rights, however, felt threatened. Since the Constitution did not restrict the power of the national government in any substantive way, they reasoned, the people in each state were at risk: at the slightest provocation, the national government could potentially swoop into a region and take control of its citizens. Since at the time of the adoption of the Constitution many people still saw states as sovereign entities, they feared any intrusion by the national government.

The states did not, however, want the Constitution to establish restrictions against the states themselves. While a "bill of rights" was desirable, its sole purpose was to guard the people against the *national* government. Thus, when the states ratified ten of the twelve amendments passed by the First Congress, now called the Bill of Rights, they were clearly understood to apply not to the states but only to Congress and the president. And in 1833 the Supreme Court ruled in *Barron v. Baltimore* that the states were not bound by the Bill of Rights.

The next major step toward uniform protection of civil liberties was the creation of the Fourteenth Amendment after the Civil War, which says that the states cannot deprive any individual of his rights without due process of law. Because this phrase, which also appears in the Fifth Amendment, is not defined in the Constitution, the Supreme Court has wrestled with its interpretation ever since the Fourteenth Amendment was adopted. In this century, the Supreme Court has applied nearly every protection in the Bill of Rights to the states through the Fourteenth Amendment.

When Tom C. Clark became a justice of the Supreme Court, much of the protection that Americans now take for granted did not exist—at least not from state governments. Many states had a bill of rights in their own constitutions; some of them even had more protections than the federal constitution. But others had much fewer; and even if states had them, if they chose to ignore their state constitutional protections there was nothing outside the state that could compel them to do so. Consequently, it did not seem unusual to people that states were not required to grant warnings to the accused at the time of arrest informing them of their rights, or to provide attorneys for defendants during trials. States without the same protection written into their own constitutions felt no obligation to follow the Fourth Amendment's prohibition of "unreasonable search and seizure," which means that agents of the federal government must have a search warrant signed by a judge (or else be in pursuit of a suspect) before they can invade a person's home and seize evidence that can be used in a trial.

Today, of course, we find nothing strange about the fact that evidence gathered without a proper search warrant, by the agent of *any* government, may not be used in court. This comes from the exclusionary rule, the legal basis on which this sweeping freedom comes. Justice Tom C. Clark had much to do with making the exclusionary rule a protection for all citizens in all legal situations; but its history went back far before he joined the Court.

In 1914, the Supreme Court ruled in *Weeks v. United States* that the Fourth Amendment means what it says: "The right of the people to be secure in their persons, houses, papers, and effects, against unreasonable searches and seizures, shall not be violated." Without following proper procedure, anything seized by the government would be invalid as evidence. The purpose of the rule was not to guarantee "fairness" for the individual on trial. Clearly, it is unfair and frustrating for everyone when the government has real evidence that conclusively proves a criminal's guilt—yet, because of the errors of police or prosecutors, such evidence can never be used. Rather, the exclusionary rule was created to guarantee a broader kind of fairness, a fairness that would be shared with the whole population. It would offer Americans a new kind of liberty, a freedom from fear of their own government invading their homes.

But since the Fourth Amendment, as part of the Bill of Rights, applied only to the federal government, the exclusionary rule could only offer Americans this freedom from fear of *federal* actions; many states continued their policies of search and seizure without judicial warrants.

This led to a strange legal situation. Because the states had only self-imposed restrictions, if any, placed on them, a criminal who committed a crime subject to both federal and state laws might be convicted in a state court because of the presence of illegal evidence but acquitted in a federal court since this evidence would have to be thrown out there.

Just before Clark came to the Court in 1949, a chance to extend this protection against state actions came in the case of *Wolf v. Colorado.* The Court agreed that the Fourth Amendment was indeed enforceable against the states through the Fourteenth Amendment. But Justice Frankfurter, speaking for the majority, claimed that the exclusionary rule was not an intrinsic part of the Fourth Amendment and that the ruling given thirty-five years earlier in *Weeks* was not necessarily demanded by the Constitution; seeing it as procedural policy for the federal courts might be a better way to look at it. This ruling had the effect of giving a green light to states to violate the Fourth Amendment, since the Supreme Court would do nothing to stop them.

Between 1949 and 1961 the composition of the Court had changed markedly. An influx of new justices brought it fresh insight on an issue that was charged with the energy of legal modernization and reform.

The case challenging *Wolf* was not a dramatic one. It started on May 23, 1957, in Cleveland, Ohio. A woman named Dollree Mapp was confronted at her home by police officers who banged on her door and demanded entrance. They believed that she was harboring a dangerous criminal who was associated with a bombing and who was possibly a subversive. It was also believed that there were items in her home related to illegal gambling. Since they had no warrant,

Mapp refused to let them inside. A few hours later, they simply broke down the door and waved a piece of paper that they claimed was a warrant (though they would not let Mapp read it). They would not allow her to talk with her attorney who had come to the house. In their thorough search, the officers found neither the suspect nor anything related to gambling—but in the basement they did find a trunk of pornographic material. Mapp claimed that a former boarder had left the trunk and that she was holding it for him. Regardless of whose it was, she claimed First Amendment free speech protection. Nevertheless, she was brought up in the Ohio courts for possessing obscene materials. She was convicted and sentenced to prison; her appeal to the Ohio Supreme Court was unsuccessful.

When the case reached the Supreme Court of the United States, no one doubted that the officers had obtained their evidence illegally. First, the warrant that they claimed to have had was of questionable validity (tellingly, it was never produced in court or anywhere else; it may have never existed), and second, if valid at all, it was only good for the two specific things mentioned above (the suspect and the gambling machines). Had the officers been agents of the United States, all evidence of the obscene material would have been excluded from the trial, but because of the *Wolf* decision the Ohio courts could admit it. Because of Mapp's case, however, the justices were able to reconsider their previous ruling; in 1961, using the Ohio case, they declared that the states were subject to the Fourth Amendment in the same way that the federal government was—through the enforcement of the exclusionary rule.

The case was decided by a six to three vote and Justice Clark was assigned to write the Court's decision. As one of the more conservative members of the majority, Clark was likely given the task of writing *Mapp v. Ohio* to prove to the nation that the decision was not one of a string of knee-jerk Warren Court liberal decisions. Rather, Clark's authorship could indicate that *Mapp* was actually based on well-reasoned doctrine that even Justice Clark, who was clearly a loyal friend of the government's interests, could join.

Clark's opinion was well developed. As a judge who liked to follow precedent, he probably had some misgivings about voting to overturn rulings that had defined the law for many years. Perhaps even harder for a conservative jurist than participating in a decision to reverse a previous ruling is to actually *write* the new opinion, and that was exactly Clark's challenge.

He wrote an opinion that took the question of the right to freedom from government intrusion back to its earliest roots. Stating that "there is no war between the Constitution and common sense," Justice Clark proceeded to point out that a constitutional command to the police to abstain from illegal searches meant nothing if it did not prohibit the use of the resulting evidence. Clark said that *Wolf* had theoretically held the national government and the state governments to the same standard on Fourth Amendment law, and they should therefore be held to the same standard on the rules of search and seizure.

Again, he reiterated that the purpose of such a rule was to stop officers from violating the Constitution. "Nothing," he wrote in the opinion, "can destroy a government more quickly than its failure to observe its own laws." Likewise, no people would long stand subject to a government that prosecuted them for breaking the law but proceeded to break the law itself.

Justices Harlan, Frankfurter, and Whittaker dissented from Clark's opinion. Their basic difference was that the Supreme Court's requirement of a proper search warrant was simply a rule that the Court handed down as the supervisor of the lower courts, not a rule absolutely required by the Constitution. One issue that Justice Clark and Justice Harlan debated was the question of applying the Fourth Amendment to the states. In a letter from Justice Harlan to

Justice Clark while the Court was still working on *Mapp*, Harlan wrote that "your opinion comes perilously close to accepting 'incorporation' for the Fourth A., and will doubtless encourage the 'incorporation' enthusiasts." Clark wrote back, saying that he did not believe "that the opinion is a windfall to 'incorporation' enthusiasts."[2] Yet, *Mapp* clearly did nationalize the scope of the Fourth Amendment. It is impossible to know how far Clark expected future decisions to use *Mapp* in the incorporation controversy over other rights, but he surely realized that *Mapp* was a milestone in that eminent development. One constitutional law guide even notes that the process of selective incorporation of the Bill of Rights "quietly began in *Mapp v. Ohio.*"[3]

Mapp v. Ohio is a case studied in history and law classes everywhere. In addition to being one of the most widely used and studied cases today, *Mapp* has provided a clear example of the Warren Court's choosing to intervene after years of inaction to protect the rights of the accused. However, although the protections *Mapp* afforded are still guaranteed, various government authorities have reduced *Mapp*'s impact over the years.

In an interesting twist of history, Dollree Mapp met up with the Clark family again several years after Justice Clark's decision had freed her in the Ohio case. Clark's son Ramsey served as her attorney—and got her off the hook again—when she had been imprisoned in New York. In a very real sense, Mapp was well served by both father and son.

Although this was probably Clark's most important written decision, another that he participated in soon afterward was the case that Earl Warren described as being the most important decided during his tenure as chief justice. *Baker v. Carr*, decided in 1962, was the famous voting equality case that came from Tennessee and reverberated throughout the legislative redistricting and reapportionment battles throughout the United States.

The case centered around the legislature of Tennessee, which had not been reapportioned since the earliest years of the twentieth century. The population trends, however, had changed significantly; more and more people were leaving the rural areas of the state and entering big cities, such as Memphis and Nashville. Thus, representatives in the state house had districts with as few as fifteen thousand people in the country, while city representatives held ten times that number. In other words, the vote of an individual on a farm could count as much as ten votes in the cities; the principle of "one man, one vote" was not present in Tennessee at all.

Representing residents of the urban areas, Mayor Charles W. Baker of Nashville brought suit against the attorney general and other officials of Tennessee. Claiming that their rights were being infringed, the citizens asked a federal court to throw out the current districting plan and institute something new and more equitable. While the issue was a burning one, a surprisingly mundane argument was used to invalidate the citizens' claims: the court ruled that the city dwellers could not sue, because federal courts were powerless over state political systems. The attorneys representing the state said that, no matter how backward a system might be, only the state itself could be held responsible for changing it. This argument is partially valid, since the Constitution clearly grants certain powers to the Congress and other powers to the states. Tom C. Clark was a proponent of this doctrine of federalism, but he also would not relinquish federal power to curb state abuses, as *Mapp v. Ohio* demonstrated.

One of the things the Supreme Court must consider when accepting cases is whether they concern "political questions." Courts cannot be used to resolve matters that pertain to the legislative or executive branches. For example, in 1849 the Court refused to consider a similar question about the political structure of Rhode Island; but the Fourteenth Amendment, which was critical in this case, had not even been imagined then. The judiciary is expected "to say what the law is" and make sure that statutes of the legislature and policies of the executive are consistent with the Constitution.

All the justices did not see the case in the same light. One group, led by Justices Frankfurter and Harlan, felt that the political nature of the problem made *Baker v. Carr* inappropriate for a court to decide. Frankfurter had, in fact, written an opinion for the Court in 1946 that stated this opinion: the "Court ought not to enter this political thicket."[4] The other faction, led by Justice Brennan, felt that the courts were empowered to decide the kind of question raised in *Baker.* Brennan's group wanted to reverse the lower court rulings. His eventual opinion in *Baker* begins with one of the most extensive explanations ever given by the Court of what kinds of cases it finds appropriate for judicial scrutiny, answering the complaints of Frankfurter's wing.

As a conservative jurist believing in states' rights, Justice Clark was originally of the opinion that the Supreme Court should stay out of the case and dismiss it altogether. In his view, the Court had been too proactive and too political in the past few years. Hence, he was aligned with the Frankfurter group.

The Court was divided five to four on the issue; Clark, Frankfurter, Harlan, and Whittaker, in the minority, argued that the issue was political. Thus, Justice Brennan would write the decision of the Court and would do it for the narrowest possible majority.

Clark, however, had not finished his consideration of the case. After initially casting his vote with Frankfurter, Clark read through the case more thoroughly. In doing research for his intended dissent, in which he had planned to show that the people of Tennessee had other ways to solve their apportionment problems than the federal courts, he was shocked to realize that in Tennessee some voting districts were unbalanced at a rate as high as nineteen to one. He concluded that the federal courts were after all the only available recourse to these people who had been denied equal protection under the Fourteenth Amendment. Thus, he changed his vote—and advocated a more sweeping decision than even Brennan demanded.

The Court was then split six to three. Views differed even within the majority. Clark wanted to address the merits of the case and actually hand down a specific solution to the reapportionment crisis. Another Justice, Stewart, was willing only to say that the courts indeed did have the power to take the case, and he wanted to send it back to the lower courts instead of having the Supreme Court decide the merits. The final decision, written by Justice Brennan, was the more conservative of the two points of view, favoring Stewart's cautious approach. In other words, Brennan did not actually solve the problem of malapportionment but declared that the issue was not, after all, simply political but was also judicial. Justice Clark wrote a concurring opinion of his own that detailed his Fourteenth Amendment reasoning. More important, Clark wrote in the opinion that he had "searched diligently for other 'practical opportunities' present under the law [but had] found none other than through the federal courts."

Interestingly, Justice Whittaker withdrew from the case because it was handed down after he had resigned from the bench. This left the opinion divided six to two.

Clark's opinion was important in several ways. First, it bolstered a shaky majority into a dominant one that could be less easily disputed by opponents. Second, it indicated that the Court would be willing to take a strong, rather than indifferent, approach to the issue of relative voting strength in the states. His opinion was, in fact, the strongest one that was handed down by any justice; later, it would prove to be useful since cases from state after state would be decided in federal courts on the same basis that Clark had stipulated.

Two other major reapportionment cases came down two years later, in 1964. Because *Baker v. Carr* was primarily a theoretical decision, it really did nothing more than assert the power of the judiciary to solve the problems, and no practical solutions were handed down. However, the new cases gave the justices a chance to say not only that there was a legal problem with uneven legislative districts but also what their constitutional remedy must be.

Reynolds v. Sims was a case from Alabama in which the basic problems of *Baker v. Carr* were replicated. Since the state legislative districts had not been redrawn since early in the twentieth century, natural shifts in population were inadequately represented in the state house. This raised two constitutional questions: first, what standard of "equal representation" must be met and, second, should it apply to *both* houses of the legislature?

The opinion that Chief Justice Warren wrote addressed the twin issues. Following a precedent established the previous year, he applied the principle of "one man, one vote," meaning that districts must not differ from each other in population size within a set limit.[5] The other question was more complicated. In Congress, the House of Representatives is based on population of the states, but the Senate is composed of two individuals from each state, regardless of how large or small the state's population may be. Each citizen in such a state as South Dakota would have the voting power of thirty-seven Californians in U.S. Senate elections. During the Constitutional Convention, the framers felt that this would stop the large states from dominating the small ones. But should the same system exist in state legislatures? Should each county be given the same number of state senators, while the house is divided among equally populated districts?

This situation at first glance seems analogous to the federal plan given in Article I of the Constitution. However, in another sense, it is different, because counties are the creation of states, while states are *not* the creation of the federal government. Counties are simply administrative subdivisions of the state government, made for convenience; this also is different from the relationship states have to the federal government. While states have some powers that Congress simply cannot take away, no such power exists for counties. In addition, such a system would be highly unbalanced, since every state has some counties that contain huge cities and others that are sparsely populated. For example, Harris County, Texas, contains Houston and has well over two million citizens, while Loving County, Texas, has just over one hundred citizens. Would it make sense to have those two counties equally represented in the state senate, with each Loving County citizen's vote equaling that of some twenty-five thousand residents of Harris County?

Some justices would not have opposed such a plan if it had been accepted by the people of the state. Chief Justice Warren, however, believed that all representatives of the people in the legislatures should be elected on a population basis. Justice Clark disagreed, writing to Warren, "I am not yet ready to join a holding striking down the federal analogy."[6] Other justices felt the same way, but the Court's ruling held that offices in the legislature must be equally distributed by population.

Clark ultimately concurred in the judgment itself, but as indicated in his letter to Warren, he was unsatisfied with a blanket rule requiring absolute numerical equality of apportionment in all cases. In *Reynolds* he wrote a separate concurrence, remarking that the majority opinion "goes much beyond the necessities of this case in laying down a new 'equal population' principle for state legislative apportionment." His argument, and rationale for concurring in the judgment, was simply that both houses of the Alabama legislature were apportioned with "invidious discrimination," making judicial intervention unavoidable—precisely the same position he had stated in *Baker v. Carr*. But, unwilling to insist, as Warren did, that "one man, one vote" *had* to be the apportionment principle of both houses of state legislatures in all cases, Clark wrote, "I, therefore, do not reach the question of the so-called 'federal analogy.' But in my view, if one house of the State Legislature meets the population standard, representation in the other house might include some departure from it so as to take into account, on a rational basis, other factors" of a state's political realities. For example, states with natural divisions created by geographical features, such as mountains or rivers, or with certain areas that are industrial and others that are rural, may wish to apportion seats in the upper house of the legislature on that kind of basis, rather than simply on population. These concerns are clearly and completely spelled out in Clark's dissent in the case of *Lucas v. Forty-Fourth General Assembly of Colorado*, decided the same day as *Reynolds*. Clark's position on apportionment in the states was a strong one, unchanged since *Baker v. Carr*: inequality in election districts was impermissible when the people have no option of changing the system except by resorting to the courts. But when such a system was basically equal, rational, and freely decided by all of the people of the state (as in a referendum), Clark did not want to interfere.

A different question concerned the population of congressional districts. In *Wesberry v. Sanders*, decided just four months before *Reynolds*, the justices were confronted with discrepancies in the district sizes in Georgia. Justice Black, writing for the majority, ruled that the districts must be of equal population. This meant that, within each state, citizens of various congressional districts would have the same voting strength. The ruling essentially ordered state legislatures, which have the duty to draw congressional district lines, to pay close attention to population.

To this day, courts are required to monitor election districts for Congress and state legislatures to make sure that, within a set percentage, the population of one does not fall short of another. Presently, courts are also observing the racial makeup of the districts as well to guarantee that no discrimination takes place because of race, any more than because of geography, socioeconomic status, or other factors.

Justice Clark's honest reversal in *Baker,* which he later affirmed in the other reapportionment cases, indicates that his approach to deciding cases was unlike the political one possibly used by other justices. He consistently reviewed the merits of each case and voted accordingly. *Baker v. Carr,* much like *Mapp v. Ohio,* was a departure from Clark's normal practice of supporting state governments. While he was willing to give them the benefit of the doubt, Clark left such preconceptions behind when individuals' rights needed protection.

* * *

The next year also proved to be of significance in the civil liberties realm. The issue of pubic school prayer had just been introduced in the case of *Engel v. Vitale.* The case was related to the First Amendment, which prohibits state establishment of religion. The establishment clause had always governed actions of the federal government. But it also pertained to the states, and since states control education, religion in the schools was bound to cause controversy.

The problem was school prayer. Could the states force students to recite a prayer without reference to a particular religion, if it presupposed God? Atheists considered this an affront and claimed that the Constitution prohibited states from participating in religion in any way. The prayer that the Board of Regents of the state of New York had approved read thus: "Almighty God, we acknowledge our dependence upon Thee, and we beg Thy blessings upon us, our parents, our teachers and our country."

The case was decided by a six to one vote, and Justice Hugo Black wrote for the majority. The state's encouragement of prayer, he said, was "wholly inconsistent with the Establishment Clause." While not a decision against religion, Black made it clear that no bias—either favoring or opposing—religion could be shown in the public schools.

Justice Potter Stewart dissented, claiming that the brief prayer was not a threat to anyone's freedom of religion. He believed that schools have a duty to instill a sense of ethics in their students; the ethical values that a school must teach could be furthered, he said, by such a prayer.

Justice Clark voted with the majority. He felt that schools were not the proper place for prayer; after all, everything must be standard, uniform, equal, and fair in a school, but not all religious beliefs are standard and uniform. When religion entered the schools, someone would inevitably lose.

One year later, in 1963, another case came before the Court that offered similar questions but with a different legal shading. If a prescribed prayer of state making was illegal, what about the Lord's Prayer, taken directly from the New Testament? And were readings from the Bible illegal? Did the fact that students, and not state employees, independently read the prayer and the verses have any bearing on the matter?

The case, *Abington School District v. Schempp,* was brought by a Pennsylvania family who protested that the law in their state encouraged religious beliefs contrary to their own. In Pennsylvania, at the time, the school day began with announcements—including the recitation of the Lord's Prayer and ten Bible verses, chosen by a student in the media class that administered the announcements. Those who could not conscientiously accept the prayer or verses were allowed to stand in the hall, but this was undesirable for two reasons. First, it ostracized them from the rest of their peers, pressuring students to disregard their principles. Second, on a more tangible level, students who elected to leave the room were not able to hear the announcements.

The Schempp family were members of the Unitarian Church. Their religious beliefs conflicted with some of the statements found in the New Testament. Because of this they feared that allowing their children to remain in class for the ten Bible verses might expose them to religious doctrines that were not in accordance with the family's views. Stating that the school district violated the children's rights by forcing them to either stand in the hall or listen to religious information, and that the district's actions ran counter to the establishment clause, the Schempps brought suit.

Both sides had compelling points of view when they presented oral arguments before the Supreme Court. The state was first to argue. It said that the activities that occurred each day in Pennsylvania schools were not an establishment of religion. Rather, they could be considered instruction in ethics, and as Justice Stewart had noted in his dissent in *Engel,* none could doubt the role of the schools in instilling ethics in their students. The state further said that the Lord's Prayer was an almost ritualistic speech that contained elements common to all religions. Finally, the state emphasized the freedom of students to exclude themselves without penalty, coupled with the majority's right to conduct business in a way that seemed fitting to them, so long as they did not actively seek to support a particular religion that was alien to the minority. The state believed that it was effectively administering majority rule without expense to minority rights.

The lawyer for the Schempps also had significant points to make. He rejected the argument the state made about the students' being excused without penalty from the announcements, because they would therefore lack information about activities on campus for the day, which was a penalty in itself. Likewise, he scoffed at the notion that the state was not establishing religion. What else, he asked, could it be doing? When praying and reading New Testament scripture is involved, it is hard to deny that Christian theology is being advocated. The scripture that the media students were able to choose could come from any part of the Bible, and many of the verses from Genesis to Revelation contained ideas and statements that would offend or contradict the teachings and beliefs of others. Any instance, for example, in which Jesus was spoken of as humanity's only chance for eternal salvation, was offensive to non-Christians. A particularly dangerous verse, the Schempps maintained, was the one in which the Jewish people received the blame for the crucifixion of Christ; this verse, they claimed, had been responsible for more persecution of Jews than anything else in the history of the world.

The Court heard the arguments made on both sides, and decided in conference that the Pennsylvania law, like the New York law, must be struck down. Justice Clark was chosen by the chief justice to write the majority opinion in the case. Clark wrote that the state government was bound, no less than the federal government, to refuse to promote one religion over another, or any religion over no religion at all. Rather than take a stand recognizing or denying religion to any extent, the justice wrote, all government in the United States must take a firm position of neutrality in any relationship between people and their God.

There was a single dissent in the *Abington* case, leading some people to say that there was only a single Bible left in the Supreme Court. Justice Potter Stewart, who had dissented in the *Engel* case, likewise dissented here. His reasoning was similar to that of his previous opinion's, as Justice Clark's reasoning was similar to the majority's in *Engel*. The major difference between the two cases was that *Engel* proscribed specific prayer ordered by the state, while *Abington* eliminated Bible reading, which included the Lord's Prayer.

The public was shocked and disappointed by both court cases. A Gallup poll suggested that three-fourths of Americans were opposed to the Court's view in the *Abington* decision. From its earliest roots, America had been a country of people with strong religious convictions. The Declaration of Independence, establishing the United States as a self-governing nation, declared that all people "are endowed by their Creator with certain unalienable Rights," and noted the signers' "firm reliance on the Protection of Divine Providence." And even today, both houses of Congress open with prayer by their chaplains. Thus, a ruling by the Supreme Court that seemed to be hostile to religion would not be well received. The public was not completely informed on the Court's decision, however. While prayer was eliminated as an official function, God had not "been taken out of the schools," as so many claimed. Clark's opinion explicitly stated that the study of religion and the Bible as literature were still available to students in the classroom setting.

Clark was a religious individual throughout his life. His son Ramsey later remarked that when his father was growing up, he "had perfect attendance records at Sunday school and all the rest."[7] But he saw religion as more than a series of rituals or a trip to church on Sunday morning. He had a personal commitment that was not determined by the confines of a single church. It was because "his religious outlook was ecumenical" that he was able to be raised Episcopalian and then join the Presbyterian Church after his marriage.[8] His legal view was clearly that the First Amendment demanded that the government and the churches be separate; but even on a practical level, he denied that the state could have any meaningful impact on a person's faith. It was for this reason, in addition to his constitutional position, that he held the conviction that religion should not be mixed with the schools—even though he was a stout adherent of Christian principles and beliefs. In fact, he said not long after the decisions were handed down that in "my day, it was the job of the parents and the preachers and Sunday school teachers to inculcate and develop a religious atmosphere among children. What we need is more people doing this and fewer passing the buck on to the public schools. One fledgling prayer leader in the home is worth a dozen parroteers in the schoolhouse."[9]

Presenting this idea to the public, Justice Clark convinced the legal profession and many citizens of the validity of the Court's position. When he wrote *Abington* after having seen the firestorm that resulted from *Engel,* his writing was marked by such "persuasive reasonableness that the decision has been almost universally accepted."[10]

One important source of support came from President John F. Kennedy, who had replaced President Eisenhower in 1961. A Roman Catholic, Kennedy nevertheless supported the Court's rulings; not necessarily because he agreed with their decisions, but because he felt that he—and all Americans—should respect the Court as having the final word on what the Constitution means. On November 22, 1963, not long after *Abington* was handed down, Kennedy was shot and killed in Dallas—Clark's hometown. Chief Justice Warren split his time over the next year between the Court and the committee he chaired (known as the Warren Commission) to investigate the assassination.

* * *

Though *Engel* and *Abington* were the most important religion decisions of the Warren Court era, others came up from time to time. Justice Clark wrote another important Supreme Court opinion on religion in *United States v. Seeger.* This case helped determine who could be a conscientious objector and consequently avoid service in the military during war because of religious beliefs. In *Seeger,* the individual claiming the status of conscientious objector did not claim belief in such a god as the deity described by Christianity, Islam, or Judaism. Instead, he claimed religious beliefs that were "based on ethical thinkers like Plato and Spinoza" but lacked any faith or belief in a specific god.[11]

The Court decided that the government could not deny Seeger his status as a conscientious objector any more than it could a devout Quaker; religious beliefs could not be "preferred" by Congress, with some deserving the reward of exemption from war but others not. In preparation for writing the opinion to be handed down in court, Clark wrote to the other justices a summary of what he believed. He wrote that "any sincere belief which *fills, in the life of the objector,* the *same place as God fills* in the life of an *orthodox religionist* is entitled to exemption under the statute."[12] This kept the case from becoming deeply embroiled in constitutional issues, while enlarging the freedom of religion for those not espousing traditional religious beliefs.

Since Clark's tenure on the Court, further challenges have been raised in the Supreme Court regarding the distinction between church and state, especially concerning the issue of school prayer. The Court has consistently stood by its previous opinions, written largely by Justice Clark, to demonstrate a firm adherence to the principles given in the First Amendment.

Proposed amendments to the Constitution that would reverse the Court's decisions have been widely debated but not passed. Recently, more than ever before, serious discussion about establishing an amendment that would guarantee students the freedom to pray individually has become increasingly popular. Some states have added, or are considering adding, provisions in state law that mandate "a moment of silence" during each school day; these laws may be challenged in the courts on the basis of past Supreme Court decisions. Their future will depend on whether the Court believes that the states wrote the laws with the intention of supporting religion.

* * *

The year after the *Abington* decision was handed down, Congress passed the Civil Rights Act of 1964. This act, passed largely in honor of assassinated President John F. Kennedy, who had strongly advocated such an act while president, strove in various ways to make the legal situation of blacks and whites more nearly equal. Title II of the act,

which was its strongest provision, established various remedies to ensure that public accommodations could not be segregated by race. This meant that any hotel, motel, restaurant, theater, or any other business or facility that either
was supported by the state or affected interstate commerce
(which, under the Constitution, Congress could regulate)
could not discriminate.

Many southern businesses, of course, had discriminated
for a long time. As the southern response to *Brown v. Board
of Education* had proven, many southerners had no intention of suddenly opening their doors to black Americans just
because the federal government said so. They would seek a
legal route to avoid the spirit of the law.

The southern business owners claimed that their entre-
preneurships were their own and that they therefore had the
right to do business with whomever they chose. Private
property could not be commandeered by the federal government, they claimed; thus, the law was unconstitutional.

But it has widely been accepted that the federal government may regulate any business as long as that business has
an impact on national or international trade. To some extent,
entrepreneurs work not only for themselves but also for the
nation as a whole. The question that business owners were
forced to ask was, "Does my establishment have a significant
impact on interstate trade?" If the answer to that question
was "yes," then the facility was forced to open to all comers.

Unfortunately for the white southerners, *their* answer to
the question was not the defining one. Federal officials, and
ultimately the Supreme Court, would answer it. The 1964 act
came right in the middle of the major civil rights push that
took place from about the time of *Brown* until approximately
the end of the Nixon administration and the Vietnam War.
Supreme Court Justice Tom C. Clark, as was shown in the
desegregation cases, was no enemy of civil rights. At the same
time, he was never a jurist who would permanently decide a
case without carefully thinking out the legal reasoning behind

any ruling. He would not make a decision contrary to his understanding of the Constitution just because a proper judgment on his part might set back the civil rights movement.

Two cases came to the Court shortly after the implementation of the Civil Rights Act; both dealt with the public accommodations section of the law. *Heart of Atlanta Motel v. United States* dealt with the requirement that lodging be color-blind. *Katzenbach v. McClung* tested the authority of Congress to require that food service be integrated for all races. As companion cases, they were decided, written, and announced together. As is usual with most companion cases, the decision that the Court reached was in principle the same for both.

In each, Justice Clark was assigned the majority opinion. As in previous cases, the decision to have Clark write the opinions—for a unanimous Court—may have had as much to do with the added psychological power he could give to the opinion due to his southern background as with anything that he could have written.

The selection of Clark to write for the Court came from Chief Justice Warren. As in all cases in which the chief justice is in the majority, it is he who chooses either to write the decision himself or to assign it to another justice who agreed with the outcome. Warren knew Clark not only as a colleague but also as a friend. After Chief Justice Warren joined the Court, Clark acquired a new morning ritual that, if not replacing the frenzied atmosphere of the executive branch of government, at least offered a smooth daily transition from family man at home to Supreme Court justice. Chief Justice Warren and his wife lived near the Clarks, and in the mornings Clark and Warren would often walk a few miles together in Washington, and then finish the trip when Warren's car picked them up at a regular spot and dropped them off at the Court. Through these walks, they could talk about pressing Court business as well as develop a personal friendship. There is no reason to doubt that discussion of

Heart of Atlanta Motel and *McClung* must have come up among the many conversations the men had. Warren, by all accounts a shrewd chief justice, must have realized not only that the Court's rulings would have more credibility if delivered by the justice from Texas but also that Clark was someone who shared the chief justice's opinions on the issue and who would write decisions that Warren could strongly support. However Warren made up his mind, he chose Clark to write the Court's answer to both cases.

It is of some interest and value to describe the decisions of both cases so that the reasoning and monumental constitutional law that they developed can be best understood. *Heart of Atlanta Motel* ended racial discrimination in hotels and motels that were important in interstate commerce. The proprietor of such a hotel that was situated along a major interstate highway running through the city of Atlanta had chosen not to serve black Americans. This business decision could be explained partly by the bias that he, as a southerner, had likely developed. But, additionally, the revenue that he could garner from whites was, to some degree, contingent upon the idea that they as customers were to be "protected" from mixing with other races. While certainly not everyone who would stay in the motel was of that opinion, enough probably wanted to stay in lodging free from black citizens to convince the owner that his economic interests would be hurt by complying with the law.

The likelihood of this possibility is doubtful; after all, if every establishment was open to every individual, there could only be an *increase* in the total amount of revenue generated across the country. Congress' motive in establishing Title II was not only to protect rights but also to spur the national economy. The motel was locally owned and not part of a national chain, but Clark wrote in the opinion that "the power of Congress to promote interstate commerce also includes the power to regulate the local incidents thereof."

Clark, writing for the majority, reminded the business owners that the Constitution explicitly gave Congress the power to regulate interstate commerce. Congress could choose to integrate major public facilities because it "possessed ample power in this regard." After all, by being denied an opportunity to spend the night, blacks were implicitly encouraged not to travel; this created burdens on interstate commerce.

Earlier in the twentieth century, the doctrine of substantive due process would have swept the government's position away as a burden on the individual right to contract with whomever one chooses and however one chooses to do it. The Court's decision was, perhaps, the final nail in the coffin of economic substantive due process and the idea that individual financial liberties are always superior to the interests of government—or the public good.

But no less important was his even more imaginative decision in the case of *Katzenbach v. McClung.* Prior to the Civil Rights Act of 1964, restaurant owners were free to serve whomever they chose; their location did not matter. Even restaurants not serving customers coming from out of state, Justice Clark ruled in sustaining the law, could contribute to interstate commerce just as hotels could.

There are two ways that restaurants can have major impacts on commerce. In a direct way, they serve people on business trips, crossing state lines, or en route to conduct some type of interstate commerce. By extension, the restaurants are themselves examples of commerce. Indirectly, restaurants participate in interstate commerce because of the food that they purchase, which may have crossed state lines.

Clark's opinion in *McClung* focuses on this last impact on commerce. The case was centered around a surprising source: a Birmingham, Alabama, restaurant called Ollie's Barbecue that served mostly local people and purchased food primarily from within the state. However, the federal issue arose because 46 percent of the food Ollie's purchased came across state lines at some point.

Ollie's played an insignificant part in interstate commerce. Nobody suggested that the national economy rested on whether the barbecue shop was open for business or not; nevertheless, the aggregate effects of discrimination at many restaurants like that one would have consequences for the economy. Discriminatory restaurants *would* serve less product from all over the United States; the amount at any particular diner was irrelevant in light of this larger perspective. Congress felt that a manufacturer in Boise, Idaho, for example, should not suffer because of racial biases held by someone in Atlanta.

The Court's ruling may seem to stretch the law; after all, few (if any) of Ollie's customers came from outside Alabama, and less than half of its food did. But Clark's opinion sustaining Congress' enormous powers of interstate commerce was not without precedent. In 1942, the Supreme Court had upheld Congress' right to govern the consumption of wheat as interstate commerce—even though the wheat had not been transported and was being eaten by the farmer who grew it.[13] Justice Clark's opinion, therefore, was new in that its result protected the civil rights of African-Americans, but it was grounded in previous Supreme Court rulings.

Justice Clark's opinions were landmarks in civil rights history not so much because they themselves produced monumental effects but because of the precedents they set. What the Supreme Court did in *Heart of Atlanta Motel* and *McClung* was give Congress the power to prescribe any civil rights remedies that it saw fit to make.

For students of Clark, this position is somewhat deceptive. At the same time that Clark was interested in giving people the right to conduct their business as they saw fit, he was also trying to preserve the proper role of the judiciary in American government. This meant deference to the policies of the other two branches when political questions were involved. In both cases, the vote was unanimous: the members of the Court who felt as Clark did could rule for civil rights because of their convictions about the role of judges in the constitutional system, while the more liberal justices could join his opinion mainly because they wanted to advance the civil rights agenda. Nonetheless, there is no doubt that "Clark consistently supported the Court's decisions to improve the legal standing of blacks." One author even isolates the year 1964 as the single most important year for Supreme Court rulings on civil rights and implies that Clark's authorship of these and other civil rights opinions were crucial to the cause.[14]

Though civil rights cases occupied much of the Court's time, it was deciding civil liberties cases as well. In 1963, a monumental decision was handed down that granted the right to counsel to all accused persons, whether in federal or in state court. *Gideon v. Wainwright* was a case in which the Supreme Court was given the opportunity to state that the Sixth Amendment right to "have the Assistance of Counsel" for one's defense meant not only that one could hire an attorney if he or she had enough money to do so but also that a lawyer would actually be provided for every defendant in every court in the country regardless of ability to pay.

The question was not new. Federal courts, for example, generally provided counsel; many state courts did as well. The rules were not clear, however, because the Supreme Court had never explicitly said when a state was required to provide counsel and when it was not required to do so. Two major decisions that were decided before Tom C. Clark entered the Court related to the right to counsel; unfortunately, they were somewhat contradictory and also rather controversial.

The first case, decided by a seven to two vote, was *Powell v. Alabama.* Handed down in 1932, *Powell* established that capital crimes, those offenses punishable by death, were so grave that judges must assign a lawyer to defend the

Shown here with his colleagues, Justice Clark would be the next to retire.(Left to right) Justices William J. Brennan, Jr., Potter Stewart, Byron R. White, Hugo L. Black, Abe Fortas, William O. Douglas, John Marshall Harlan II, Chief Justice Earl Warren, Justice Clark. Taken between late 1965 and summer 1967.

<small>FROM THE TOM C. CLARK PAPERS, TARLTON LAW LIBRARY, UNIVERSITY OF TEXAS AT AUSTIN</small>

accused in all cases. It implied that, were the charges serious enough, states should provide an attorney for a defendant; however, no clear rule defining a sufficiently serious crime was established beyond the circumstance of a case involving a possible death penalty.

Ten years later, the Court decided *Betts v. Brady.* In that case, a Maryland defendant had requested a lawyer in his state trial and was denied one. The Supreme Court ruled that the Sixth Amendment's provision for counsel was not covered by the Fourteenth Amendment and thus each state could form its own rules, so long as the *Powell*-type exceptions were maintained. Nevertheless, prior to *Gideon*, a number of cases before the Court seeking special exceptions had been decided, invariably for the defendant—but on a case-by-case basis, never by virtue of an all-encompassing constitutional rule.

In *Betts*, Justice Hugo Black was a vocal dissenter; he believed that the entire Bill of Rights was incorporated against the states by the Fourteenth Amendment. He was still on the Court when *Gideon v. Wainwright* was argued and, not surprisingly, was still hostile to the state's point of view. But he also thought that the states would actually benefit by a new rule that would require the presence of counsel; this benefit would come into play because there would no longer be the possibility of reversal in appellate courts as had happened many times before Gideon's case.

The story of the defendant in the case, Clarence Earl Gideon, is told in the book *Gideon's Trumpet* by Anthony Lewis. This book was also made into a movie, which is shown in government classrooms throughout the United States. The book is of rare quality; it presents, in the form of a novel, the story of one of the most dramatic and important recent Supreme Court cases.

Clarence Gideon's story is neither dramatic nor important. He was a regular American who had regular problems. His crime was unromantic: he was accused of breaking into a poolroom and stealing a pocketful of quarters from a vending machine. Yet his story led to a right that is shared by all defendants, from rapists and murderers to petty lawbreakers.

Gideon was arrested based on the testimony of a witness who claimed to have been waiting for transportation across the street. At the time of arrest, Gideon's pockets were indeed full of quarters. He was brought into court and was expected to defend himself. But instead he requested an attorney. Claiming, "the United States Supreme Court says I am entitled to be represented by counsel," Gideon made it clear that he expected the trial judge to provide one.[15] The Florida judge rejected this. Under the prevailing law, the judge was probably correct. The rule at that time was defined by *Betts*, and since Gideon was not charged with murder (in which case the *Powell* ruling would have given him a lawyer), he really had no legal ground on which to stand. Perhaps it was his bad luck to be coming to trial in a southern state; most northern states at the time provided counsel.

After being informed that his request was denied, Gideon attempted to examine witnesses as best he could. His performance was not that of a skilled lawyer, naturally, and later it was noted that he did not use key points that could have helped establish his innocence. Not surprisingly, he was convicted and sentenced to prison (because of previous conviction, his sentence was particularly long).

Imprisoned and despondent, but never doubting that justice was on his side, Gideon began a strenuous appeals process. He tried to obtain relief from the Supreme Court of Florida, but that court refused his appeal. Then Gideon began his crusade to have the U.S. Supreme Court review his case.

Since Gideon had no attorney (this being the whole purpose of the litigation, in fact), the Court appointed Abe Fortas—soon to become a member of the Court—to represent him. Both Fortas and the lawyer in the Florida attorney general's office, who was charged with defending Florida's law, began working feverishly to prepare the briefs and materials necessary to conduct a successful case before the nation's highest tribunal.

Fortas, arguing for Gideon, told the justices that it was foolish to think that an individual could competently represent himself when lawyers were required to undergo years of training before they could represent someone else. He criticized the Court's decision in *Betts,* saying that it was not only inconsistent with the pattern established in *Powell* but also logically incompatible with the Sixth and Fourteenth Amendments. Not only did Fortas ask that Gideon's conviction be reversed, he also asked the Court to reverse its own ruling in *Betts v. Brady.*

The state disagreed. Relying heavily on the doctrine of federalism, Florida argued not only that it had the constitutional right to choose whether or not to grant attorneys but also that as a sovereign state it could actually do away with all attorneys. The entire system of justice in the state courts was subject only to the basic notion of due process.

The Court took the arguments of counsel and decided unanimously that *Betts* should be overruled. Hugo Black, who had opposed the Court's position for so long, was given the especially pleasant role of being able to write the opinion reversing it. His relatively brief majority opinion focused on the errors the Court had made in deciding *Betts.* Black believed that, by establishing the principle of *Gideon,* the Court was returning to the sound policies that were initiated by *Powell* over thirty years earlier.

Justice Clark wrote a concurring opinion that explained why he felt that the Court's judgment was the correct one. His opinion was simple but eloquent, written almost in the form of a logical syllogism. He first stated that there is no constitutional difference between a case that results in the death penalty and a case that has some other punishment. The Constitution, he wrote, "requires due process of law for the deprival of 'liberty' just as for deprival of 'life.'"

85

Next, Clark pointed out that the Constitution must be internally consistent. If it is dedicated to protecting liberty as well as life, as he said that it was, it only made sense that the same procedures would be used. In other words, the Court could not "tolerate a procedure which it condemns in capital cases on the ground that deprival of liberty may be less onerous than deprival of life."

The justice finally said that the two constitutional doctrines—that liberty must be protected with as much rigor as life and that constitutional procedures for such protection must be equivalent—were not consistent with the status quo. After *Powell* and *Betts*, capital crimes received special protection, while noncapital crimes did not. This distinction, Clark wrote, must be "erased," and this basis alone was enough to cause him to concur with Black's judgment.

The problem of adequate legal representation for those unable to afford their own attorney was not new to Clark. Four years before *Gideon* was decided, he delivered a speech to a group of lawyers in Minneapolis, Minnesota. Referring to in forma pauperis applications (literally, "as a poor person") to the Supreme Court—the kind used by Clarence Gideon— he declared: "I would like you to interest yourselves in them. . . . They plague the Court. . . . The petition is usually *pro se,* a lawyer rarely participating. This lack of counsel at the petitioning stage is most unfortunate and stands as a blot on our profession."[16] What Clark asked lawyers to do here, he and the rest of the Court forced them to do in *Gideon.*

Gideon received a new trial in Florida. With the assistance of counsel, he was able to show that he was innocent of the crime he was accused of and left the court system a free man.

* * *

Issues like those championed by Clarence Earl Gideon, the urban citizens of Tennessee, and Dollree Mapp were and still are important. Justice Clark did not participate in the decisions of many of today's controversial legal questions, but he may have left some thoughts or comments in earlier cases about those issues. It is impossible to know what Justice Clark "would have thought" had he still been on the Supreme Court when the later cases came along, but when he did leave specific writings, his beliefs about such issues can at least be surmised.

One issue that Justice Clark wrote about was cameras in the courtroom. Today, it is common to see clips from a trial on the news. Everyone saw parts of the O. J. Simpson murder trial; there is even a television network now that is devoted solely to taping and showing what goes on in courtrooms in America. But this is a recent phenomenon. The Supreme Court is not allowed to be taped or filmed; and until the past few years, the same rule applied in every court. This was, in fact, a legal rule established by Justice Clark in the case *Estes v. Texas*. Clark was not "antipress," however; he wrote in his opinion that the media "has been a mighty catalyst in awakening public interest in governmental affairs. . . . While maximum freedom must be allowed the press in carrying on this important function in a democratic society its exercise must necessarily be subject to the maintenance of absolute fairness" for the defendant. He therefore searched for a balance between the rights of the press and the right to an unbiased hearing before a court. He believed, and wrote in his opinion, that television was detrimental to a fair trial and that, because a trial was taped, the defendant's rights would be violated. He thought that those involved in a trial would likely act differently if they knew they were being taped than if no one outside the courtroom would see their actions. Therefore, he would not allow reporters to bring in their cameras, but he would allow reporters to be present at the trial and tell their audiences what they had seen. Newspaper reporters, he noted, could not bring their typewriters into court; neither should network news journalists be allowed to film proceedings.

But we cannot assume that this would be Clark's opinion forever. As he wrote in his opinion of the case, "When advances in these arts permit reporting by printing press or television without their present hazards to a fair trial we will have another case." Others think that "Tom Clark would be appalled" at the current situation—in which cameras are allowed in hundreds of courtrooms around the country.[17] He certainly was in 1965.

Another quagmire that entangled America not long after Clark left the Court was the issue of drugs. But he did cast a vote in a drug-related case. *Robinson v. California* caused the Court to consider whether or not being addicted to drugs was a crime. The Court's decision was that addiction could not be considered a crime because it was a mental illness. Justice Clark rejected this argument and dissented.

Justice Clark did, of course, participate in a number of Supreme Court cases that extended the rights of the accused. One vote he cast is worth noting because it was in such a famous case: *Miranda v. Arizona.* This was the opportunity the Court took to ensure that the accused are made aware of their rights. The famous "you have the right to remain silent" speech that the police give to criminals comes from this case. Clark dissented; he believed that the Court's ruling was unlikely to help police and local government protect the community from crime.

One final prominent issue is reproductive freedom. Justice Clark was on the Court when *Griswold v. Connecticut* was decided. In *Griswold,* the Court ruled that married individuals had the right to obtain contraception and be counseled about family planning. Clark wrote to the other justices, "There's a right to marry, maintain a home, have a family. This is in an area where we have the right to be let alone."[18]

Griswold was one of the strongest bases the Court used in writing *Roe v. Wade,* the case legalizing abortion. Judging by Justice Clark's thoughts, one might be inclined to think that he would have upheld abortion rights. But this is not necessarily the case; justices' votes cannot be predicted in that manner. Justice Potter Stewart, for example, voted in the minority in *Griswold*—saying that the state *could* prohibit contraception—but voted in the majority in *Roe*—saying that the state could *not* prohibit abortion. Similarly, Justice Byron White was in the majority in *Griswold* but dissented in *Roe*.

Throughout his tenure as a justice of the U.S. Supreme Court, Justice Clark never forgot the high purpose for which he had been chosen. In some cases he ruled for the government, as in *Jencks, Watkins, Barenblatt, Heart of Atlanta Motel,* and *McClung.* In other cases he decided for the individual, as in *Youngstown, Brown, Cooper, Mapp, Baker, Abington,* and *Gideon.* Clark's decisions were never made for a specific group or a specific ideology; they were made for the American people at large. His judicial opinions were valued because of their clarity and logical poise; his personal opinions were valued because they were *his.* Although his career as a justice started in a shadow of doubt, he left the Supreme Court as a widely respected jurist whose departure was met with public and private sadness.

CHAPTER FIVE

AFTER THE

SUPREME COURT

Justice Clark turned sixty-seven in September 1966. He was in tip-top condition; his mind was still at its peak and his body was in fine form. However, he began to think that his time might be better spent with his family and in other less time consuming pursuits than as a justice of the U.S. Supreme Court.

What finally caused him to leave the Court was, indeed, family related. His son, Ramsey, was a rising star in the Justice Department. When Attorney General Katzenbach became Secretary of State, Ramsey Clark became the most likely individual to succeed him in the top job, the same position his father had held under President Truman less than twenty years before. As a liberal, Ramsey Clark had become well known in the administration, and President Lyndon Johnson announced in early 1967 that he had indeed chosen the younger Clark to be the attorney general.

Having once been attorney general himself, Justice Clark recognized that it would not be easy for his son, as the nation's highest lawyer, to have a father as a Supreme Court justice. The federal government is involved in a tremendous

*As President Lyndon Johnson watches, Justice Clark swears in his
son, Ramsey, as Attorney General of the United States,
the position Tom Clark himself once held, March 1967.*
FROM THE TOM C. CLARK PAPERS, TARLTON LAW LIBRARY,
UNIVERSITY OF TEXAS AT AUSTIN

number of cases that come before the Court each year; thus,
the attorney general is a lawyer in a significant number of
those cases. This seemed to pose a conflict of interest. How
would it appear to the public to have a father judging his
son's cases? Since so many Supreme Court rulings were
decided by a bare majority, with the margin of a single vote,
it is not hard to imagine the pressure that the Clarks felt. Of
course, the justice could decline to participate in any case
he wished. This would, however, have been unfair to the
American people who were paying for and deserved a full-
time judge. Clark was constitutionally guaranteed lifetime

tenure, so only he could decide what course of action should be taken. Because he wished to avoid even the appearance of impropriety, he chose to announce that, at the end of the term, he would retire as a justice of the Supreme Court.

This was a striking decision. By choosing to retire, he gave up the rest of his lifetime on the nation's highest court so that his son could serve in the executive branch for what would turn out to be less than two years. Ramsey Clark commented on this during his eulogy of his father ten years after the decision had been made. He said that "Tom Clark was a giver. He gave what once seemed to me too much: career, power, prestige—the work of a lifetime—cut off prematurely as he retired from the Supreme Court. He never discussed it. He never even mentioned it. Instead, he turned to things like traffic courts and for three years he labored that the good people of this land brought before municipal courts would see principle possessed there, truth found and applied in their cases."[1]

Ramsey Clark's tribute alludes to the major focus of his father's last ten years, efforts at forging new judicial reforms throughout the country. But there was also an irony in the eulogy's memory of Justice Clark's sacrifice for his son. The Clarks' situation corresponded to—in reverse—a similar one that occurred less than forty years before Clark resigned. Charles Evans Hughes's son served under President Hoover as solicitor general, the third-ranking member of the Justice Department, who was the lawyer in charge of presenting the government's positions to the Supreme Court. This position is perhaps the most prestigious job for a practicing lawyer. Yet, in 1930, President Hoover offered Hughes the position of chief justice, and in this case, the *son* resigned so that the *father* could serve on the Supreme Court.

But Clark's retirement was not particularly painful. Mary, however, seemed sad to leave the community of the Court; she looked disappointed at a private party that they hosted at the Supreme Court on Clark's last day on the job.

The day that a Supreme Court justice leaves the Court is rare. Not only are there so few justices, but they each generally serve for many years as well. In fact, most of them leave only upon death or when death is imminent. Few, like Clark, have retired in their prime. Thus Clark was able to continue to interact with the legal establishment after he left the Court.

When Clark retired, President Johnson chose to appoint Solicitor General Thurgood Marshall, a former federal appeals court judge, to fill the vacancy on the Court. Marshall was well known as the lawyer who represented the National Association for the Advancement of Colored People in various cases before the Supreme Court, including *Brown v. Board of Education.* Clark and Marshall were thus not strangers; in fact, their relationship went back even further than the *Brown* case. After Clark's death, Marshall was quoted in the *New York Times* as praising him for filing the brief with the Supreme Court in the 1948 racial covenant case: "This act was doubly important because it was the first brief by an Attorney General in support of civil rights, and it was ordered by a man from Texas."[2] Marshall, who until 1991 served in the seat Clark had once held, was the nation's first African-American justice.

At the time of his retirement, Clark was seen to be "an able jurist who had grown during his 18 years on the bench and who had become a very productive member of the Court, writing some of its most important opinions."[3] Professor Charles Alan Wright of the University of Texas, Clark's law school, spoke at the memorial ceremony at the Supreme Court after Clark died. He said that "Clark left an enduring legacy . . . in opinions that will shape American law beyond any of our lifetimes."[4] The importance and relevance of a justice can be measured in terms of how long his or her decisions remain the law of the land; Tom C. Clark will always live in such cases as *Mapp, Baker, Abington,* and *Heart of Atlanta Motel,* as their underlying philosophies continue to shape American history and policy.

Justice Clark in retirement, as Senior Judge, in judicial gown, 1970.
FROM THE TOM C. CLARK PAPERS, TARLTON LAW LIBRARY,
UNIVERSITY OF TEXAS AT AUSTIN

The discussion of Clark's service on the Supreme Court should be recognized as only one part of a full life. Clark never did retire from law, since after leaving the high court he sat as a judge in every circuit court of appeals in the country and was the first person to do so. He spent an increasingly strenuous amount of time heading court reform efforts and serving as the leader of numerous organizations designed to improve knowledge about the judiciary. After years of producing many lengthy opinions each year, he also easily became a prodigious writer, composing numerous law review articles during his retirement years.

Clark's career was clearly far from over when he left the Court. Some have indicated that, his major Supreme Court decisions notwithstanding, a number of the greatest contributions he made to America came in his so-called retirement.

The most important thing to Justice Clark at the end of his life was the nationwide reform of the courts. Any discussion of the many organizations and boards on which he served must be somewhat selective because there were so many. Such a discussion must also be incomplete, because there is so much to say. Furthermore, any discussion must be out of chronological order, because he belonged to so many simultaneously. Yet there must be a discussion, because perhaps more than any other man this century, Justice Clark was an instigator of positive and tangible judicial reform. Strangely, the public has hardly recognized his offerings; but as Justice Lewis Powell once commented in a remarkable tribute, "it is likely that Mr. Justice Clark was known personally and admired by more lawyers, law professors, and judges than any justice in the history of the Supreme Court of the United States."[5]

Between the years when Justice Clark retired from the Court and when he died, only two articles were written about the major role he played in court reform. The latter of these two is a paper written by James A. Gazell and published in the *Houston Law Review*. His article deals in depth with the statistics, facts, and ideas behind the justice's long-term involvement in reform. While most of this is beyond the scope of a brief biography, several points are interesting to note.

The first thing that one must realize about Justice Clark is that there is a strong distinction between his role as a justice and his role as a reformer. As a justice Clark dealt with specific laws and doctrines while, as a judicial reformer, he focused on the machinery of justice. Even those who mildly opposed some of his court decisions have called him "the traveling salesman of justice," "the country's most distinguished expert of state judicial administration," and "the Father of Modern Judicial Administration."

What organizations would someone described as the "Father of Modern Judicial Administration" be involved in throughout a career? A sample from Gazell is provided: "the Joint Committee on the Administration of Effective Justice and its successor, the Coordinating Committee on Effective Justice; the National Conference of State Trial Court Judges; the National College of State Trial Court Judges; the Institute of Judicial Administration; the Twenty-Seventh Columbia University Assembly; the A.B.A.'s [American Bar Association] Special Committee on Evaluation of Disciplinary Enforcement; and the A.B.A.'s Criminal Justice Standards Implementation Committee. His efforts with the last two groups continued into the early 1970s, which also saw him serve as chairperson of the National Conference on the Judiciary."[6] This list is incomplete. Nonetheless, the image of influence and prestige that such a list provides is staggering.

For a man who was a Supreme Court justice, most of whom were isolated in the ivory tower of the Court in Washington, a desire to develop state courts was surprising. In the years 1962 and 1963 alone, he spoke to more than two-thirds of all state trial judges in the country, a significant number of individuals. The pace did not diminish after retirement.

Even when he was unable to focus on judicial reform because of his duties as a member of the Court, Justice Clark's Herculean efforts were far from unnoticed. In the early 1960s, the prestigious National Lawyers Club honored Justice Clark in a tangible way. The club displayed only two portraits: one of the founder of the organization and the other of Justice Clark. This was a tremendous honor for a living individual, especially a sitting judge. When asked to explain, the organization stated that it hung the portrait of the justice at its doors "so that all might see as they come in the man who best exemplifies the finest career in Government."[7]

As a justice he was "principally responsible" for organizing the National College of State Trial Judges (which later became the National College of the State Judiciary). With its headquarters in Colorado, Clark participated in as many functions as he could, flying often to Boulder to address groups. This was, perhaps, the association he was most excited about.

He concerned himself not only with state courts but also with city courts. He founded the National Conference of Metropolitan Courts, which printed a remarkable tribute to him upon his death. This conference was dedicated to the improvement of justice in the nation's giant cities, just as the National College of State Trial Judges and the Institute for Court Management were useful in governing other courts.

The interest that Clark had in state and local courts was matched by his desire to improve federal courts. Congress established and funded the Federal Judicial Center the year that Clark retired from the Court; Clark was considered the foremost proponent of the Center and was credited with its establishment. The center was needed to modernize the almost ancient system of district courts in the United States; a central governing or advisory body would be more than beneficial. And, coincident with his retirement, it was no surprise that Tom C. Clark was made the first director.

Clark is more recognized for his work with the Federal Judicial Center than for any other aspect of his reform efforts.

In his extensive paper, Gazell quotes Chief Justice Warren's pleasure at Clark's acceptance of the position of the first director of the Federal Judicial Center, which was established by Congress (with support from Earl Warren) as a way to provide training and information to the federal court system. Describing Clark, Warren said,

> No person of our nation is better qualified to form such a Center. It is almost as though his entire career had been preparing him for the mission of the Center. A private practitioner in Texas, a prosecutor and Attorney General of the United States, a Justice of the Supreme Court, an organizer and Chairman of the massive operations of the Joint Committee for Effective Justice, President of the Institute of Judicial Administration and Chairman of the Board of the American Judicature Society, he has for many years devoted himself to the administration of the courts. The Center under Mr. Justice Clark is guaranteed the finest possible leadership. When in September of 1969 this Center's first director reaches seventy and must retire we can be assured that it will be established on a firm foundation.[8]

Clark was instrumental in the establishment of the National Judicial College, similar to the National College of the State Judiciary. This organization is an intense training and retraining program for federal judges; jurists throughout the country continue to be reeducated by the college yearly.

Clark believed that proper justice could only come from proper judges. Although it is rare to think of judges being punished, Clark strongly advocated systems that would apply tough standards to a judge if he or she were ethically corrupt or professionally incompetent. Part of this, Clark felt, came from the idea of selecting all judges by merit,

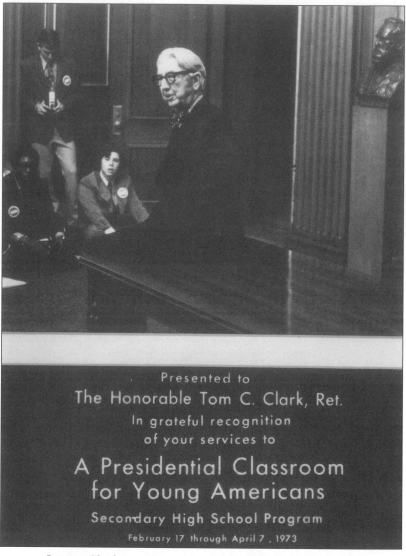

Presented to

The Honorable Tom C. Clark, Ret.

In grateful recognition
of your services to

A Presidential Classroom
for Young Americans

Secondary High School Program

February 17 through April 7 , 1973

*Justice Clark in retirement, sharing his thoughts on the
judicial system with high school students in the
Supreme Court building, 1973.*
FROM THE TOM C. CLARK PAPERS, TARLTON LAW LIBRARY,
UNIVERSITY OF TEXAS AT AUSTIN

rather than election. As the Chairman of the Board of the American Judicature Society, Clark fervently advocated various means of choosing judges for competence rather than political expediency. In coordination with the same group, he realized that lawyers could occasionally fall from high standards. Thus, "the subject of lawyer discipline probably had no stronger champion than Justice Clark."9

Clark's interest in the courts went beyond the mere mechanics of administration. He was also a student of the rich history of the Supreme Court, much of which he himself had made. In 1974, one of the premiere organizations in the academic study of the Court was founded—the Supreme Court Historical Society. Justice Clark was chosen to be the first chairman of the board of trustees: an honor and a responsibility. It is partly to his credit that the society has progressed as far as it has; it is a shame that he was not able to live long enough to see the prestige of the organization grow.

Justice Clark never gave up his judicial role. Until the day he died, Clark traveled across the country in the position of senior judge, filling in at trial and appellate courts in the federal system. This was his way of contributing to his system of justice. When a particular court was becoming backlogged, he was there. When the Supreme Court held its memorial ceremony after his death, Chief Justice Warren E. Burger, who had replaced Earl Warren in 1969, made the comment that "there was no problem that reached my desk on which he was not prepared and willing to shoulder responsibility at my request. . . . No one in the history of this Court, after retirement as an associate justice, has ever engaged in such constant and steady judicial activity, as well as continuing his missionary work."10

But as a retired justice, Clark was also able to spend more time than ever before on personal matters. He had worked hard to remain personally in touch with numerous relatives and friends during his busy years as a government

101

official. According to his family, he was never without paper and pen when there was any kind of spare time available—watching television, listening to music, waiting for an appointment, or riding on an airplane. Anxious never to waste any time, Clark would jot brief notes to many people on any variety of subjects. The notes functioned primarily to maintain his personal connection with their recipients. Receiving a handwritten letter, however short, from someone as busy as a Supreme Court justice communicated more than the note's contents; it expressed the fact that Clark cared about that person and was thinking of him or her even with his hectic schedule. Many of those notes were lost or destroyed, but many of them remain. Upon retirement, Clark had even more time for such pleasant chores.

And of course the Clarks were able to indulge in travel more frequently. Because none of Clark's activities—numerous as they were—were as rigid or tied to a specific schedule as the routine of a justice, the Clarks could spend time in places and ways that they had never before been able to do. When they were at home in Washington, they acted like ordinary citizens and guarded their privacy. Clark particularly enjoyed being a grandfather and often baby-sat his grandchildren.

A story known to few people helps to indicate how much the Clarks prized both privacy and the chance to live like "normal people" in retirement. Several years after he left the Court, when Clark was in his early seventies, he decided one afternoon to walk from his apartment to a nearby drugstore to purchase a few things. It was not terribly far from home, although it was a good walk; apparently, he had done this before. When he left the store, a pair of assailants followed him a short way and then mugged him. They obviously had been watching him in the store, because they knew exactly where he had placed his wallet and immediately took it away from him and ran off. Justice Clark, outraged, chased after them, shouting; but he was naturally slower than they were and eventually he lost track of them. Apparently, Clark did not report the incident

Retired Justice Clark addressing secondary students, 1973.
FROM THE TOM C. CLARK PAPERS, TARLTON LAW LIBRARY,
UNIVERSITY OF TEXAS AT AUSTIN

and it was certainly not an item for the news. The wallet he brought to the store contained only a small amount of money; his driver's license, credit cards, and other essentials were back at the apartment. It is hard to imagine the publicity that would have been spawned if he had been seriously harmed or murdered—it would have shocked the American public for a retired Supreme Court justice to be killed on the streets of Washington close to his home in broad daylight. But Clark, valuing his privacy, did not spread the story.

Neither Tom Clark, known always as the "Texan" wherever he went, nor his wife, Mary, ever lived in Texas after 1937, although they visited often. But they maintained their ties with the state through their actions and words and thoughts.

103

The death of Justice Clark was obviously a great loss to many. His health had been declining for several years, but he would not reduce his workload despite Mary's pleas to do so. Many people have accordingly said that he "died with his boots on." He was in New York City, working as a judge of the Second Circuit Court of Appeals. On the evening of June 12, 1977, Justice Clark was at the New York home of his son Ramsey, who was out of town at the time, studying the case he was to hear the next day. He had laid out his papers upon a coffee table and then retired to bed. At some point in the night, he passed away.

Justice Clark's death was a sad occasion for many—for his family, friends, fellow judges, and those citizens whom he had helped. President Jimmy Carter ordered the American flag to be flown at half-mast at American installations throughout the world. Judges and other public officials offered praise for Clark at the time of his death. Chief Justice Warren Burger said that "no one in the past 30 years has contributed more to the improvement of justice than Tom Clark." In the pamphlet by the National Conference of Metropolitan Courts, a Florida judge said that Clark "was truly the 'Patron Saint' of America's trial courts."[11]

Perhaps the most personal and touching tribute to Justice Clark came from his son, Ramsey, in his eulogy. Justice Clark's son said that his father "knew that the true joy of life is being exhausted in a cause you yourself deem mighty." He noted that his father "never had so high a commitment to any ideology that he ever permitted it to distract from his love for people." And he concluded his remarks by saying, simply, that "I believe Tom Clark is the best man I've ever known." Years later, Ramsey Clark remembered his father's life as an amazing one, filled with energy and passion. Commenting on the statement that "life's unfair," he said that "if you took Tom Clark's life, you'd have to say, 'Life's unfair. His was too good.'"[12]

At one point in his life, Tom Clark had made a comment about the kind of person he liked. Today we can use that comment to describe Clark himself. He liked "men who prefer honor to wealth, truth to sophistry, kindness to covetousness, modesty to vaingloriousness, service to recognition, humility to grandeur, usefulness to reward."[13]

* * *

NOTES

CHAPTER 1

1. Mary Clark, Mimi Clark Gronlund, and Tom Gronlund, personal interview by author, 24 November 1995.
2. C. B. Dutton, "Mr. Justice Tom C. Clark," *Indiana Law Journal* 26 (1951): 170.
3. Ramsey Clark, "Remarks," in *A Symposium on the Tom C. Clark Papers* (Austin: University of Texas, 1987), 30.
4. Mimi Clark Gronlund, "Tom Clark: The Formative Years" (master's thesis, George Mason University, 1984), v.
5. *This Honorable Court*, pt. 1, prod. WETA-TV, Greater Washington Educational Telecommunication Association, 1988, video, interviewing Joseph Rauh Jr.
6. Maisie Conrat and Richard Conrat, *Executive Order 9066* (Los Angeles: California Historical Society, 1972), 44.
7. Tom Clark, "Epilogue," in *Executive Order 9066*, by Maisie Conrat and Richard Conrat (Los Angeles: California Historical Society, 1972), 110.
8. Robert M. Langran, "Tom C. Clark," in *The Supreme Court Justices*, ed. Clare Cushman (Washington, D.C.: Congressional Quarterly, 1993), 426; and Bernard Schwartz, *Super Chief* (New York: New York University Press, 1983), 16.
9. Tom Clark, "Epilogue," 111.

CHAPTER 2

1. Tom C. Clark, "Reminiscences of an Attorney General Turned Associate Justice," *Houston Law Review* 6 (1969): 626.

2. Mimi Clark Gronlund, "Tom C. Clark, 1899–1977," in *A Symposium on the Tom C. Clark Papers* (Austin: University of Texas, 1987), 25; and John P. Frank, *The Warren Court* (New York: Macmillan, 1964), 95.

3. William H. Chafe, *The Unfinished Journey*, 3rd ed. (New York: Oxford University Press, 1995), 62; and Ronald Reagan, *Speaking My Mind* (New York: Simon and Schuster, 1989), 179.

4. "Communists Assail Truman at Rally," *New York Times*, 20 September 1946, 3.

5. "Truman Aid Asked in Communist Fight," *New York Times*, 24 April 1947, 3.

6. Lewis Wood, "Ninety Groups, Schools Named on U.S. List As Being Disloyal," *New York Times*, 5 December 1947, 1, 18.

7. Lewis Wood, "'Freedom Train' to Start Sept. 17," *New York Times*, 23 May 1947, 5.

8. "Political Aim Seen in 'Freedom Train,'" *New York Times*, 3 June 1947, 22.

9. "Lynch Issue to Go to Supreme Court," *New York Times*, 25 May 1947, 46.

10. "How to Measure Loyalty," *New York Times*, editorial, 12 May 1947, 20.

11. "Banquet Complimenting the Hon. Tom C. Clark, Attorney General of the United States" (Texas State Society of Washington, D.C., 29 May 1946, banquet program).

CHAPTER 3

1. Clark, "Reminiscences of an Attorney General," 624.

2. Ibid.

3. Bernard Schwartz, *A History of the Supreme Court* (New York: Oxford University Press, 1993), 254, 256, quoting Fred Rodell, *Nine Men* (New York: Random House, 1955), 311.

4. Clark, "Reminiscences of an Attorney General," 626.

5. Gronlund, "Tom Clark," 71.

6. David M. O'Brien, *Storm Center: The Supreme Court in American Politics*, 3rd. ed. (New York: Norton, 1993), 121–22.

7. Dutton, "Mr. Justice Tom C. Clark," 174.

8. *This Honorable Court.*

9. O'Brien, *Storm Center,* 347.

10. Tom C. Clark, interview by Robert Ireland, Washington D.C., 8 May 1973, in *Fred M. Vinson Oral History Project,* University of Kentucky Library.
11. Tom C. Clark and Philip B. Perlman, *Prejudice and Property* (Washington, D.C.: Public Affairs Press, 1948), 84.
12. John D. Fassett, "Mr. Justice Reed and *Brown v. the Board of Education,*" in *Yearbook* (Washington, D.C.: Supreme Court Historical Society, 1986), 57.
13. Earl Warren, *Memoirs of Earl Warren* (Garden City, N.Y.: Doubleday, 1977), 4.
14. Clark, Gronlund, and Gronlund, interview.
15. Gronlund, "Tom Clark," v–vi.
16. Schwartz, *Super Chief,* 57, 138.
17. Richard Kirkendall, "Tom C. Clark," in *The Justices of the United States Supreme Court,* vol. 4, ed. Leon Friedman and Fred L. Israel (New York: Chelsea House, 1980), 2665.
18. Ibid., 2671.
19. *Tileston v. Ullman.*
20. Kirkendall, "Tom C. Clark," 2672.

CHAPTER 4

1. Clark, Gronlund, and Gronlund, personal interview.
2. Schwartz, *Super Chief,* 396–97.
3. Jerome A. Barron and C. Thomas Dienes, *Constitutional Law* (St. Paul, Minn.: West, 1986), 115.
4. *Colegrove v. Green.*
5. *Gray v. Sanders.*
6. Schwartz, *Super Chief,* 506.
7. Ramsey Clark, "Remarks," 32.
8. Mimi Clark Gronlund, letter to author, 7 December 1995.
9. Charles Alan Wright, "Remarks," in *In Memoriam: Honorable Tom C. Clark* (Washington, D.C.: Supreme Court of the United States, 1978), 20.
10. Frank, *The Warren Court,* 79.
11. Schwartz, *Super Chief,* 570.
12. Ibid., 572.
13. *Wickard v. Filburn.*
14. Langran, "Tom C. Clark," 429; and Kirkendall, "Tom C. Clark," 2675.

15. Anthony Lewis, *Gideon's Trumpet* (New York: Random House, 1964; reprint, New York: Vintage Press, 1989), 10 (page citations are to the original edition).
16. Tom C. Clark, "How Cases Get into the Supreme Court," in *An Autobiography of the Supreme Court*, ed. Alan F. Westin (New York: Macmillan, 1963), 298.
17. Gregory Curtis, "TV on Trial," *Texas Monthly* (July 1995): 6.
18. Schwartz, *Super Chief*, 578.

CHAPTER 5

1. Ramsey Clark, "Tom Clark Eulogies," in *Yearbook* (Washington, D.C.: Supreme Court Historical Society, 1978), 5–6.
2. "Tom C. Clark, Former Justice, Dies; On the Supreme Court for 18 Years," *New York Times*, 14 June 1977, 38.
3. Catherine A. Barnes, "Tom C. Clark," in *Men of the Supreme Court: Profiles of the Justices* (New York: Facts on File, 1978), 59.
4. Wright, "Remarks," 23.
5. *In Memoriam: Honorable Tom C. Clark* (Washington, D.C.: Supreme Court of the United States, 1978), 38.
6. James A. Gazell, "Justice Tom C. Clark As Judicial Reformer," *Houston Law Review* 15 (1978): 309.
7. Frank, *The Warren Court*, 94.
8. Gazell, "Justice Tom C. Clark As Judicial Reformer," 326.
9. Arlin M. Adams, "Tom C. Clark: Certified Champion of Justice," *Judicature* (Sept. 1977): 101.
10. *In Memoriam*, 50–51.
11. "Tom C. Clark, Former Justice, Dies," 1; and *Memorial Tribute of the National Conference of Metropolitan Courts to Its Distinguished Founder* (pamphlet, 1977).
12. Ramsey Clark, "Tom Clark Eulogies," 5–6; and Ramsey Clark, "Remarks," 30.
13. Frank, *The Warren Court*, 96.

GLOSSARY

antitrust—legislation against or in opposition to trusts, specifically consisting of laws to protect trade and commerce from unlawful restraints and monopolies or unfair business practices

appellate court—a court having the power to review the judgment of another court

argue—to present evidence in a court of law before a judge, as in "to argue a case"

associate justice—a member of the Supreme Court, other than the chief justice

attorney general—the chief law officer of a nation or state who represents the government in litigation and serves as its principal legal adviser

Bill of Rights—the first ten amendments to the U.S. Constitution, summarizing the fundamental rights and privileges guaranteed to a people against violation by the state

chief justice—the presiding or principal judge of the Supreme Court

civil liberties—freedom from arbitrary government interference with one's rights, especially those political in nature guaranteed by the First Amendment

civil rights—the nonpolitical rights of a citizen, especially the rights of personal liberty guaranteed to U.S. citizens by the Thirteenth and Fourteenth Amendments of the Constitution and by acts of Congress; freedom from discrimination by government and other citizens

Cold War—the ideological conflict between the United States and the Soviet Union

concurring opinion—an opinion of one or more justices that agrees with the main ruling of the Court

conscientious objector—a person who refuses to serve in the armed forces on moral or religious grounds

constitutional law—the area of the law that deals with the interpretation of the Constitution, the nation's primary source of law; the law that sets rules for government actions

dissenting opinion—an opinion of one or more justices that disagrees with the main ruling of the Court

due process—formal legal proceedings carried out regularly and in accordance with established rules and principles

eminent domain—a right of the government to take private property for public use

establishment clause—a statement in the First Amendment that prohibits the government's establishing or endorsing a religion

exclusionary rule—the legal doctrine stating that evidence obtained in violation of Fourth Amendment protections cannot be used in court. It was made binding against the states in *Mapp v. Ohio.*

executive order—a rule or order issued by the president and having the force of law

federalism—the distribution of power between the national and state governments, usually referring to states' rights

First Amendment—the amendment to the Constitution guaranteeing Americans the freedom of speech, religion, the press, assembly, and the right to petition the government

Fourteenth Amendment—one of three constitutional amendments resulting from the Civil War; it extends national citizenship rights to all Americans and prohibits the states from violating these rights. The Supreme Court has often used its due process clause to guarantee that state governments do not violate the Bill of Rights.

Fourth Amendment—the constitutional amendment that protects people's property from government intrusion, searches, or seizures without a proper warrant

incorporate—to apply an amendment, or part of an amendment, of the Bill of Rights to a state

in forma pauperis—as a poor person

injunction—an order by a court requiring someone to do or refrain from doing a specified act

integration—the ending of segregation, by bringing all races together as equal members of society; requiring schools and other public places to accept individuals of all races

judicial reformer—one who works to improve the legal system of courts of law

law clerk—a justice's assistant, who helps in reading documents, doing research, and writing drafts of judicial opinions

machine politics—politics controlled by a political party organization, usually at the city or county level, but sometimes at the state level, and headed by a "boss" or a small group of leaders. A political machine may use bribery, patronage, illegal manipulation of elections, or other dishonest means to stay in power.

New Deal—the legislative and administrative program of President Franklin Roosevelt, designed to promote economic recovery and social reform during the 1930s

oral argument—hour-long presentations to the Supreme Court for a case, split equally between the parties to the lawsuit

pack (the court)—President Roosevelt's plan to increase the size of the Supreme Court and fill the Court with justices who were sympathetic to his views

pro se—on one's own behalf; representing one's self, without the assistance of a lawyer

reapportionment—the redrawing of district lines so that each district contains approximately the same amount of voters

relocation centers—camps in the interior part of the United States in which Japanese-Americans from the West Coast were forced to live during World War II because of extreme public fear of the Japanese after the attack on Pearl Harbor. This policy was ordered by President Franklin D. Roosevelt.

segregation—the separation of races by enforced or voluntary residence in a restricted area, by barriers to social intercourse, by separate educational facilities, or by other discriminatory means

share—when a business is divided into equal portions, each portion is called a share. The shares are then bought by individuals to help finance the cost of the business.

Sixth Amendment—the constitutional amendment guaranteeing certain rights to those accused of crimes, including the right to a speedy, public trial; the right to a fairly chosen jury; the right to be informed of the nature of the accusation; the right to confront witnesses; and the right to the assistance of a lawyer

solicitor general—the Justice Department attorney, subordinate to the attorney general, whose primary responsibility is to represent the government in the Supreme Court

sovereign—independent, as the states are independent of the national government

stare decisis—a policy of following rules or precedents laid down in previous judicial decisions unless they go against the ordinary principles of justice

statutes—laws enacted by the legislative branch of a government

substantive due process—a judicial requirement that laws may not result in the unfair, arbitrary, or unreasonable treatment of an individual, usually used to protect economic freedoms

subversive activities—a systematic attempt to overthrow or undermine a government or political system, often by persons working secretly from within

BIBLIOGRAPHICAL ESSAY

There is an enormous body of literature about the Supreme Court in general, but very little is available about Justice Tom C. Clark in particular. In this essay, I will identify those references I find particularly relevant to a study of Clark's life, as well as some especially good sources that explain the context of Clark's career—particularly books and articles that deal with major cases in which Clark participated. Many of these can be found in public school libraries; almost all are readily accessible at a local university library.

TOM CLARK AS AN INDIVIDUAL

Very little has been written about Tom Clark's life. As far as I can tell, this is actually the first book dedicated as a biography of Justice Clark. There are a number of books, however, that contain brief biographical sketches of all the justices of the Supreme Court. Catherine A. Barnes's *Men of the Supreme Court: Profiles of the Justices* is a good overview of the Court, although it is out of date for justices after John Paul Stevens (Sandra Day O'Connor and those following her are missing). A more recent book, which is composed of articles by many different authors, is *The Supreme Court Justices*, edited by Clare Cushman. This is as good a source as I have found on a number of the more obscure justices; the essay on Clark is by Robert M. Langran and runs from pages 426 to 430.

A biographical essay that is far more focused on Clark's legal career is Richard Kirkendall's essay in *The Justices of the United States Supreme Court*, volume 4, edited by Leon Friedman and Fred L. Israel, from page 2665 to page 2677. Kirkendall's essay gives a good overview of Clark's work on the Supreme Court. In this book I have discussed a number of the most important cases that he mentions briefly.

After Clark's death, a memorial service was held in the Supreme Court building. Transcripts of the speeches given have been printed by the government in a booklet entitled *In Memoriam: Honorable Tom C. Clark.* Clark Clifford (pp. 11–16) spoke about Clark up until he became a justice; Professor Charles Alan Wright (pp. 16–24) spoke about Clark's work on the Supreme Court; and Fred Vinson Jr. (pp. 24–29) spoke about Clark's work to improve the judicial system. Following these speeches is the transcript of proceedings by the Court to approve resolutions honoring Clark; this includes comments by then Attorney General Griffin Bell and Chief Justice Warren E. Burger. Ramsey Clark also presented one of the Tom Clark Eulogies, in the 1987 *Yearbook* of the Supreme Court Historical Society.

Clark's family heritage was discussed in Florence Knight Fruth's *Some Descendants of Richard Few of Chester County, Pennsylvania, and Allied Lines.* His own family has written and spoken about Clark as well. The best source available anywhere about Clark's early life is the thesis by his daughter, Mimi Clark Gronlund, "Tom Clark: The Formative Years." Unfortunately, it is as yet unpublished, but it still can be found if one tries hard enough; it is, for example, in the stacks of the law library of the University of Texas at Austin. Mimi Clark Gronlund also wrote, and orally presented, "Tom C. Clark, 1899–1977," which appears in *A Symposium on the Tom C. Clark Papers*, pages 22–25. In the same publication, Clark's son Ramsey presented his "Remarks" on pages 27–33. These essays, as well as others in *A Symposium*, were collected when the Clark papers were formally dedicated at the University of Texas. These papers are the complete files that Justice Clark kept during his years on the Supreme Court, and they have been an invaluable resource to students not only of Clark himself but also of the Warren Court and of general American history during the 1950s and 1960s. Any student of the Court who can afford the time to visit there will feel a tingling sense of excitement, as I did, when he or she lifts and reads outlines of famous decisions written in Clark's own handwriting.

Throughout this period many articles in national newspapers also documented the role Clark played in the national government, both as attorney general and Supreme Court justice. I particularly recommend the *New York Times*, which has been used in this study.

CLARK IN THE DEPARTMENT OF JUSTICE

There is less written work available about Clark's four years (1945–1949) as attorney general of the United States than any other adult period of his life. The *New York Times* makes frequent reference to him when major issues, such as the Freedom Train or the problem of Communists in government, arose. Some sources that have much to say about his years on the Supreme Court also deal with his career in the Justice Department, albeit less fully. One text, *Executive Order 9066*, by Maisie Conrat and Richard Conrat, details the internment of Japanese-Americans during World War II, a policy with which Clark was familiar because of his official role in it. Clark actually wrote the epilogue to this book.

Truman, by David McCullough, is one of the best biographies of President Truman and therefore mentions Clark in passing as Truman's attorney general and nominee to the

Supreme Court. However, in such a long and complete book, one can only be surprised and dismayed at how infrequently Clark is mentioned, rather than the reverse.

Shortly after his retirement, Justice Clark wrote "Reminiscences of an Attorney General Turned Associate Justice" in the *Houston Law Review.* This is an interesting account of how Clark transitioned (as a number of other justices have) from the high-visibility role of attorney general to the almost "monastic" life of a justice.

Finally, although it is a source available to few individuals, the display case at Tom C. Clark High School has several nice visual sources about Clark's years as attorney general. They include photographs as well as a banquet program for a dinner hosted by the Texas State Society of Washington, D.C., honoring Clark for becoming attorney general.

CLARK ON THE SUPREME COURT

Clark's role as a justice is more fully documented in some publications, but Clark himself is almost never a primary focus of a book. One exception is Frances Howell Rudko's *Truman's Court,* which contains chapters on all of the justices appointed by President Truman and conceptualizes their impact on the Court as a whole. I especially recommend it to anyone studying the Vinson Court era (1946–1953); it also has more information on Clark than most books about the Supreme Court and has been gratefully consulted with frequency in the course of this study. Jan Palmer's *The Vinson Court Era* is basically a catalogue of voting patterns of all the justices during Vinson's tenure as chief justice, which is probably not useful to the average reader. However, the introductory remarks are very thorough and would be interesting to anyone wanting a sense of what Court operation was like during this time.

Clark began his tenure on the Vinson Court and was originally considered to be something of a "clone" of Fred

Vinson. His first year on the Court is analyzed from this perspective in C. B. Dutton's "Mr. Justice Tom C. Clark," in the *Indiana Law Journal.*

Of particular usefulness for the human interest side of the Supreme Court presided over by Earl Warren (1953–1969) is *The Warren Court,* by John P. Frank. Including outstanding photographs, the essays on each of the justices in this book are fun, easy to read, and quite informative. A few comments by Hugo L. Black and Elizabeth Black in their *Mr. Justice and Mrs. Black* shed light on the personality of Clark and his wife, Mary; this book is a collection of the diaries of Elizabeth Black and brief memoirs by her husband, Justice Hugo Black. The memoirs of another colleague also reveal personal thoughts about Clark; Earl Warren's *Memoirs of Earl Warren* is especially interesting on account of Warren's comments about the Southern justices' role in *Brown v. Board of Education.*

Particular cases in which Clark played a role are the subjects of much documentation as well. Gregory Curtis's "TV on Trial," in *Texas Monthly,* is an interesting glance back at the decision Clark wrote (*Estes v. Texas*) that outlawed the presence of recording cameras in courtrooms; this decision has of course since been reversed. One of the best books about a Supreme Court case is *Gideon's Trumpet,* by Anthony Lewis. This book vividly traces the case of Clarence Earl Gideon (*Gideon v. Wainwright*), through which the Supreme Court guaranteed all Americans accused of a crime the right to be represented by a lawyer even if they are too poor to afford it. The book is beautifully written by an outstanding author who is today still a close watcher of the Supreme Court.

THE SUPREME COURT AS AN INSTITUTION

Other sources take a more general approach to the work of the Court. Bernard Schwartz, a well known Supreme Court scholar, wrote two books that have been extremely useful in this study and to many who have studied the Court: *A History of the Supreme Court* and *Super Chief*. The former is a general history of the Court that is relatively easy to read and quite complete. The latter is an exhaustive look at the Supreme Court during the Warren years; it may even be the authoritative history of the Court during that time. I have found none better.

There are several other good sources on Supreme Court and constitutional history that are worth consideration for anyone interested in studying any part of American legal history. A nicely illustrated and brief text is *Equal Justice under Law*, by Mary Ann Harrell and Burnett Anderson. This text is an outstanding guide for readers of all ages about the importance of the Supreme Court. A guide for instructors is available should its use in class be desired. *The American Constitution*, 7th edition (in two volumes), by Alfred H. Kelly, Winfred A. Harbison, and Herman Belz, is one of the most complete histories of American constitutionalism. It is not just a history of the Supreme Court; rather, it traces constitutional government in the United States back to the first European settlements. It is really a complete American history text, but one written through the perspective of American law; it is aimed at high school and college students.

The Court and the Constitution, by Archibald Cox, former solicitor general and Harvard professor, is a general overview of the role of the Supreme Court in American government. The current chief justice, William H. Rehnquist, wrote *The Supreme Court*. Not only is it a good source on the Supreme Court in American history (written by someone who has played a major role in it himself), but it is particularly useful as well regarding the steel seizure case (*Youngstown v. Sawyer*) discussed in this book. Rehnquist was a Supreme Court clerk during the time that decision was handed down.

David M. O'Brien's *Storm Center: The Supreme Court in American Politics*, refers to Justice Clark on numerous occasions in his study of the Supreme Court's role in politics.

O'Brien's work is primarily aimed at providing a glimpse into the operations and inner workings of the Court, rather than at being a historical narrative. Similar is Lawrence Baum's *The Supreme Court,* which refers to Clark on occasion but is primarily useful to the reader wanting a more informed and pragmatic understanding of what it is the Supreme Court actually does.

A fine video that is highly recommended for classroom use is *This Honorable Court,* part 1, produced by WETA-TV. It is a well-done survey of Supreme Court history that introduces students to the many-faceted role that the Court has played in American life. If part 1 is perfect for a history class, part 2 would be a useful tool in a government or civics classroom; relying on interviews with current justices, it explains—like Baum's text does—the internal functioning of the Court.

Understanding the role of the Supreme Court in history implies the existence of a historical context in which Supreme Court cases were decided. Any good text on American history will be a valuable aid to the student of the Court; not understanding the Gilded Age would make understanding substantive due process almost impossible, for example. A good source on America's political traditions and history is the three volume *Encyclopedia of American Political History,* edited by Jack P. Greene. This text presents detailed articles about many important concepts in United States political history; since, as Tocqueville noted, most political problems are ultimately resolved as judicial questions, it would be a useful reference. A more general, but extremely well written and thorough, history of the United States focusing on the period in which Clark was attorney general and Supreme Court justice is William Chafe's *The Unfinished Journey.*

Understanding the Supreme Court necessarily involves understanding its decisions; besides issuing written judgments, it has no other way to influence the country or the law. There are numerous books that attempt to help a reader gain knowledge of Supreme Court opinions. Some, such as *The Supreme Court and the Constitution*, edited by Stanley I. Kutler, contain abridgments of a number of the most important cases along with introductory comments to each. Edward S. Corwin's *The Constitution and What It Means Today*, is a legal classic that takes each provision of the Constitution, one by one, and proceeds to give a complete history of how the Court has interpreted that provision through its cases. David P. Currie's *The Constitution of the United States: A Primer for the People* and *Constitutional Law*, by Jerome A. Barron and C. Thomas Dienes, are guides that explain Supreme Court decisions in the context of major "themes" of constitutional law. Of these two, Currie's is aimed at secondary and college students, and even the general public, while the book by Barron and Dienes is part of the West Nutshell Series, aimed principally at law students.

However, the best way to understand the Supreme Court, and especially the cases one is interested in, is to actually read the cases as written by the justices. All Supreme Court actions are printed in *U.S. Reports*, which can be found at any college library and many public libraries. Included in this book's bibliography is a list of all Supreme Court opinions discussed in the text. These citations refer to the location of the actual opinion in *U.S. Reports*. Take, for example, *Gideon v. Wainwright*, 372 U.S. 335 (1963). This citation means that the case of *Gideon v. Wainwright* is in volume 372 of *U.S. Reports* and starts on page 335, and was decided in the year 1963. Readers will find it a pleasant surprise that most opinions, especially for the major cases, are not difficult to read at all—they certainly do not contain the technical "legalese" one might expect. It would not be a waste of time for even middle-school students to try to read a case after they have studied it in this book or elsewhere. All readers are encouraged to visit *U.S. Reports*, because that is the final, ultimate, and authoritative word about each case.

CLARK'S EXTRAJUDICIAL WORK

Besides being a Supreme Court justice, Clark was an advocate for judicial reform and efficiency. This primarily occupied the last ten years of his life, after he had retired from the Supreme Court. His writing, on this topic and other topics relating to his work as a jurist, is quite prolific.

Several articles Clark wrote will be of special interest to students. "How Cases Get into the Supreme Court," in *An Autobiography of the Supreme Court,* is an interesting discussion of the topic by someone uniquely situated to answer it. Already mentioned have been Clark's articles about moving from the attorney general's office to the Supreme Court and his epilogue to the book about the relocation of Japanese-Americans during World War II. He also wrote, with Philip B. Perlman, *Prejudice and Property.* This was his brief to the Supreme Court in the case of *Shelley v. Kraemer,* in which he opposed segregation in the form of restricting residency of certain houses to whites.

Others wrote about Clark as well, focusing primarily on his role as judicial reformer. Two particularly useful articles are James A. Gazell's "Justice Tom C. Clark As Judicial Reformer" in the *Houston Law Review,* and Arlin M. Adams, "Tom C. Clark: Certified Champion of Justice" in *Judicature.* A symbolic tribute to Clark's efforts at improving the system of justice in the United States came at his death in the publication of a lengthy brochure entitled *Memorial Tribute of the National Conference of Metropolitan Courts to Its Distinguished Founder.* I saw this in the Clark High School display case. I am unsure of where else one would find it, but its existence is a testimony to the respect Clark enjoyed as an advocate of judicial change.

BIBLIOGRAPHY

COURT CASES

Abington School District v. Schempp, 374 U.S. 203 (1963).

Baker v. Carr, 369 U.S. 186 (1962).

Barenblatt v. United States, 360 U.S. 109 (1959).

Barron v. Baltimore, 32 U.S. 243 (1833).

Betts v. Brady, 316 U.S. 455 (1942).

Brown I v. Board of Education of Topeka, 347 U.S. 483 (1954).

Brown II v. Board of Education of Topeka, 349 U.S. 294 (1955).

Colegrove v. Green, 328 U.S. 549 (1946).

Cooper v. Aaron, 358 U.S. 1 (1958).

Engel v. Vitale, 370 U.S. 421 (1962).

Estes v. Texas, 381 U.S. 532 (1965).

Gideon v. Wainwright, 372 U.S. 335 (1963).

Gray v. Sanders, 372 U.S. 368 (1963).

Griswold v. Connecticut, 381 U.S. 479 (1965).

Heart of Atlanta Motel v. United States, 379 U.S. 241 (1964).

Jencks v. United States, 353 U.S. 657 (1957).

Katzenbach v. McClung, 379 U.S. 294 (1964).

Korematsu v. United States, 323 U.S. 214 (1944).

Lucas v. Forty-Fourth General Assembly of Colorado, 377 U.S. 713 (1964).

Mapp v. Ohio, 367 U.S. 643 (1961).

Marbury v. Madison, 5 U.S. 137 (1803).

Miranda v. Arizona, 384 U.S. 436 (1966).

Plessy v. Ferguson, 163 U.S. 537 (1896).

Powell v. Alabama, 287 U.S. 45 (1932).

Reynolds v. Sims, 377 U.S. 533 (1964).

Robinson v. California, 370 U.S. 660 (1962).
Roe v. Wade, 410 U.S. 113 (1973).
Shelley v. Kraemer, 334 U.S. 1 (1948).
Tileston v. Ullman, 318 U.S. 44 (1943).
United States v. Seeger, 380 U.S. 163 (1965).
Uphaus v. Wyman, 360 U.S. 72 (1959).
Watkins v. United States, 354 U.S. 178 (1957).
Weeks v. United States, 232 U.S. 383 (1914).
Wesberry v. Sanders, 376 U.S. 1 (1964).
Wickard v. Filburn, 317 U.S. 111 (1942).
Wolf v. Colorado, 338 U.S. 25 (1949).
Youngstown Sheet & Tube Co. v. Sawyer, 343 U.S. 579 (1952).

BOOKS, ARTICLES, PERSONAL COMMUNICATIONS, AND OTHER REFERENCES

Adams, Arlin M. "Tom C. Clark: Certified Champion of Justice." *Judicature* (Sept. 1977): 101, 135–36.

"Banquet Complimenting the Hon. Tom C. Clark, Attorney General of the United States." Texas State Society of Washington, D.C. 29 May 1946. Banquet program.

Barnes, Catherine A. "Tom C. Clark." In *Men of the Supreme Court: Profiles of the Justices.* New York: Facts on File, 1978.

Barron, Jerome A., and C. Thomas Dienes. *Constitutional Law.* St. Paul, Minn.: West, 1986.

Baum, Lawrence. *The Supreme Court.* 4th ed. Washington, D.C.: Congressional Quarterly, 1992.

Black, Hugo L., and Elizabeth Black. *Mr. Justice and Mrs. Black.* New York: Random House, 1986.

Chafe, William H. *The Unfinished Journey.* 3rd ed. New York: Oxford University Press, 1995.

Clark, Mary, Mimi Clark Gronlund, and Tom Gronlund. Personal interview by author. Washington, D.C. 24 November 1995.

Clark, Ramsey. "Remarks." In *A Symposium on the Tom C. Clark Papers.* Austin: University of Texas, 1987.

———. "Tom Clark Eulogies." In *Yearbook.* Washington, D.C.: Supreme Court Historical Society, 1978.

Clark, Tom C. "Epilogue." In *Executive Order 9066*, by Maisie Conrat and Richard Conrat. Los Angeles: California Historical Society, 1972.

———. "How Cases Get into the Supreme Court." In *An Autobiography of the Supreme Court*, edited by Alan F. Westin, 291–98. New York: Macmillan, 1963.

———. Interview by Robert Ireland, Washington, D.C., 8 May 1973. In *Fred M. Vinson Oral History Project*, University of Kentucky Library.

———. "Reminiscences of an Attorney General Turned Associate Justice." *Houston Law Review* 6 (1969): 623–29.

Clark, Tom C., and Philip B. Perlman. *Prejudice and Property*. Washington, D.C.: Public Affairs Press, 1948.

Conrat, Maisie, and Richard Conrat. *Executive Order 9066: The Internment of 110,000 Japanese Americans*. California Historical Society Series, no. 51. San Francisco: MIT Press, 1972.

Corwin, Edward S. *The Constitution and What It Means Today*. 14th ed. Revised by Harold W. Chase and Craig R. Ducat. Princeton, N.J.: Princeton University Press, 1978.

Cox, Archibald. *The Court and the Constitution*. Boston: Houghton Mifflin Company, 1987.

Currie, David P. *The Constitution of the United States: A Primer for the People*. Chicago: University of Chicago Press, 1988.

Curtis, Gregory. "TV on Trial." *Texas Monthly* (July 1995): 5–6.

Cushman, Clare, ed. *The Supreme Court Justices*. Washington, D.C.: Congressional Quarterly, 1993.

Dutton, C. B. "Mr. Justice Tom C. Clark." *Indiana Law Journal* 26 (1951): 169–84.

Fassett, John D. "Mr. Justice Reed and *Brown v. the Board of Education*." In *Yearbook*. Washington, D.C.: Supreme Court Historical Society, 1986.

Frank, John P. *The Warren Court*. New York: Macmillan, 1964.

Fruth, Florence Knight. *Some Descendants of Richard Few of Chester County, Pennsylvania, and Allied Lines*. Parsons, W.V.: McClain, 1977.

Gazell, James A. "Justice Tom C. Clark As Judicial Reformer." *Houston Law Review* 15 (1978): 307–329.

Greene, Jack P., ed. *Encyclopedia of American Political History*. 6 vols. New York: Charles Scribner's Sons, 1984.

127

Gronlund, Mimi Clark. Letter to author, 7 December 1995.

———. "Tom C. Clark, 1899–1977." In *A Symposium on the Tom C. Clark Papers*, 22–25. Austin: University of Texas, 1987.

———. "Tom Clark: The Formative Years." Master's thesis, George Mason University, 1984.

Harrell, Mary Ann, and Burnett Anderson. *Equal Justice under Law.* Washington, D.C.: Supreme Court Historical Society, 1988.

In Memoriam: Honorable Tom C. Clark. Washington, D.C.: Supreme Court of the United States, 1978.

Kelly, Alfred H., Winfred A. Harbison, and Herman Belz. *The American Constitution.* 2 vols. 7th ed. New York: Norton, 1991.

Kirkendall, Richard. "Tom C. Clark." In *The Justices of the United States Supreme Court,* edited by Leon Friedman and Fred L. Israel. Vol. 4. New York: Chelsea House, 1980.

Kutler, Stanley I., ed. *The Supreme Court and the Constitution.* 3rd ed. New York: Norton, 1984.

Langran, Robert M. "Tom C. Clark." In *The Supreme Court Justices,* edited by Clare Cushman. Washington, D.C.: Congressional Quarterly, 1993.

Lewis, Anthony. *Gideon's Trumpet.* New York: Random House, 1964. Reprint, New York: Vintage Press, 1989.

McCree, Wade H. "Remarks." In *In Memoriam: Honorable Tom C. Clark.* Washington, D.C.: Supreme Court of the United States, 1978.

McCullough, David. *Truman.* New York: Simon and Schuster, 1992.

Memorial Tribute of the National Conference of Metropolitan Courts to Its Distinguished Founder. Pamphlet. 1977.

O'Brien, David M. *Storm Center: The Supreme Court in American Politics.* 3rd ed. New York: Norton, 1993.

Palmer, Jan. *The Vinson Court Era.* New York: AMS Press, 1990.

Pritchett, C. Herman. *Civil Liberties and the Vinson Court.* Chicago: University of Chicago Press, 1954.

Reagan, Ronald. *Speaking My Mind.* New York: Simon and Schuster, 1989.

Rehnquist, William H. *The Supreme Court.* New York: Quill, 1987.

Rodell, Fred. *Nine Men.* New York: Random House, 1955.

Rudko, Frances Howell. *Truman's Court.* New York: Greenwood Press, 1988.

Schwartz, Bernard. *A History of the Supreme Court.* New York: Oxford University Press, 1993.

———. *Super Chief.* New York: New York University Press, 1983.

This Honorable Court. Pt. 1. Produced by WETA-TV. Greater Washington Educational Telecommunications Association, 1988. Video.

Vinson, Fred M., Jr. "Remarks." In *In Memoriam: Honorable Tom C. Clark.* Washington, D.C.: Supreme Court of the United States, 1978.

Warren, Earl. *Memoirs of Earl Warren.* Garden City, N.Y.: Doubleday, 1977.

Wright, Charles Alan. "Remarks." In *In Memoriam: Honorable Tom C. Clark.* Washington, D.C.: Supreme Court of the United States, 1978.

INDEX

W

Wallace, Henry, 15

War Frauds Unit, 14

Warren Commission, 74

Warren Court, 38, 42, 56, 60, 62, 74

Warren, Earl, 38, 41–43, 44, 50, 55, 62, 66–67, 74, 77–78, 99, 101

Washington, D.C., 8, 9, 10, 12, 14, 17–18, 20, 49, 56, 77, 97, 102–103

Watkins v. United States, 49–52, 53, 89. *See also* Congress: and Communism

Weeks v. United States, 58–59. See also *Mapp v. Ohio*

Wesberry v. Sanders, 68. *See also* Supreme Court: and reapportionment

Whittaker, Charles E., 53, 61, 64–65

Wolf v. Colorado, 59–61. See also *Mapp v. Ohio*

World War I, 2, 10, 11

World War II, 13–14, 20, 22, 37

Y

Youngstown Sheet & Tube Company v. Sawyer, 33–37, 89, 120

ABOUT THE AUTHOR

Evan Young has accomplished the remarkable: written a well-researched, readable biography about the only born and bred Texan ever to serve on the United States Supreme Court—while still a high school and college student.

Young has been fascinated by the nation's highest court since he was a small child. As a student at the San Antonio, Texas, high school named for Justice Tom C. Clark, he

wrote a paper about the Justice for a senior English class project. Interest whetted about Clark's career, and challenged because little had been written about him, Young took on the daunting task of research to write this book. *Lone Star Justice: A Biography of Justice Tom C. Clark*, is the first book about Justice Clark.

For Evan Young, however, the remarkable seems almost routine.

Young, whom one teacher called "perhaps the smartest student I have ever seen," was valedictorian of the Clark High School Class of 1995, where he served as chapter president of the National Honor Society and was named a National Merit Scholar. He also earned two state championships, in American Government and Essay, at the prestigious Texas Academic Decathlon.

He went on to study at Duke University, majoring in history, and also studied for a year at Waseda University in Tokyo, Japan. Young's goals are to teach constitutional law at a major law school, serve on a federal appeals court—and perhaps someday to add another distinguished Texan to the Supreme Court.